What Most Women Don't REALIZE

A Message of Wisdom, Love, Hope, and Prosperity!

Ruby J. Davis

What Most Women Don't Realize

Copyright © 2009 Ruby J. Davis

ISBN: 978-1-935125-49-5

Book printed in the United States of America

To order additional copies of this book go to:
www.rp-author.com/Davis

Rp

Robertson Publishing
59 N. Santa Cruz Avenue, Suite B
Los Gatos, California 95030 USA
(888) 354-5957 • www.RobertsonPublishing.com

Dedication

I would like to dedicate this book to all the women in the world that are not aware of the part that they might have played in a failed relationship or marriage. And to realize that being single is not a curse, it is a gift from GOD. If we, as single women, can embrace being single we will be able realized the unwise choices and mistakes that we made, wanting to be in a relationship or marriage just because we didn't want to be alone. Marriage is supposed to be the most wonderful thing on earth that GOD has designed for two people to enjoy. But when we do not follow the guidelines that GOD has given us to allow it to work, this is what causes the failure and many divorces. It took me three dedicated relationships (marriages) to realize that the problem was not me nor them the problem was that nobody loved GOD first, so therefore nobody knew how to love each other.

GOD has given us guidelines to follow and until will chose to follow them it will never work properly. There is a reason GOD gave us instructions for a successful marriage and if we didn't follow his instructions this is the reason you are not happy today and now you are taking it out on everyone else that you meet or come in contact with and the only person to truly blame is yourself, not the world. Stop being angry at the world for choices that you made, we all make our own choices. We also have to be prepared to live with the consequences that comes along with the choices that we decided to make. If you can change your situation then you change it but if you can't change it live with it and be happy, stop being so angry to innocent people that had nothing to do with who you choose to marry or be with.

Table of Contents

Acknowledgements

TO

GOD

I have to give thanks to GOD for allowing me to live and be able to share my life struggles and involvements in wrong relationships and dealings with the wrong people while on my journey so I can help someone else to not make the unwise choices and same mistakes that I made. Thank you GOD for giving me the reassurance every day of my life that you are always with me no matter what.

ME

I was blind but now I see. Thank GOD for loving, saving and delivering me. As long as I know GOD is with me everything will always be alright, the sky is the limit and no weapon formed against me shall PROSPER.

A Special Thanks

TO

<u>My Children</u>

To my only two children, my daughter Kathyrn and my son Sammie Jr. Both of you mean the world to me. It gives me such great pleasure just to hear your voices. Thanks for growing up and realizing that mommy always did the best I could for the both of you with whatever I had and tried to make your life better in whatever way that I could. I will always love the both of you from the bottom of my heart.

Introduction

RISE UP ~ BE YOURSELF

I have been single the last six years of my life, ever since my last husband left me. He got up, got dressed for work and went out the door and I have not seen or heard from him since. This was the best thing that he ever did for me since we had been married, which was leave me with no forwarding address. This was truly a blessing in disguise but GOD has always been looking out for me doing for me what I could not do for myself. I have to truly thank GOD for that every day I wake up. For twenty years of my life I was always trying to accommodate and love men that didn't even love themselves, nor did they love GOD. Making sacrifices and doing everything in my power trying to make something work that was never meant to be, trying to be a loving wife, how GOD created me to be.

Through it all, I can't be mad at anyone nor hold anger and bitterness in my heart because of the unwise choices that I made in my life. But I can truly say thank GOD for delivering me from half-grown men and allowing me the opportunity to do it his way so I can get it right. I have learned so much throughout my journey dealing with half-grown men that didn't know their left from right until I have to be thankful that there is a GOD. I don't look at those years as a waste of time because GOD will give me double for all of my troubles and I can enjoy what GOD has promised me here on earth which is peace and happiness. If I had not had the opportunity to be entangled in those bad, unfit, unhealthy relationships I would never know what a good one is suppose to be like. I would like to thank all the men who thought I was just a fool that really didn't know any better, for helping make me become the women that I am today. I hope someday that men get this in their head that they are not getting over on women, they are only getting over on themselves because at the end of the day when they think they got it all going on, they will get back everything they ever done to us and then some. We all will have to reap the seeds that we have sown. So ladies, don't worry just sit back and relax! no evil deed goes unpunished.

Chapter 1

Being Single and Embracing It

I never knew that being single was so great!!! I have finally experienced no mess, no stress from unfit, unhealthy relationships. I have spent the last six years of my life single and I have to admit it is truly a gift from GOD. Being single is a blessing not a curse, it is healing time for the body, soul and mind and preparation time. I didn't realize what precious gift I was missing, as a single women I have been able to conquer everything that I have put my hands on without any unnecessary static and drama in the background. It feels so great to make my own decisions and spend as much time as I want with GOD without having to explain to anyone. For many years I thought I had to be in a relationship for different reasons but at this point in my life none of the reasons made sense because I was never satisfied nor happy or content in the relationships. Since the day I became fully and totally single I can truly say that I cheated myself for many many years of my life; I haven't had the simple things in a marriage or relationship, such as a healthy and productive conversation, backrub, or even a walk in the park, not even a honeymoon! But that is okay because GOD has already promised me double for all my troubles. I am not disappointed nor holding any anger or bitterness in my heart toward anyone who tried to make my life miserable because they didn't know who or what they wanted. I just want to thank them for allowing me to realize the best is yet to come and I can move on to the best that GOD has for me. The best is always saved for last and I am waiting on just that.

I encourage single women to stop letting men take advantage of you when you know he doesn't want you. Until we decide to stand up for something we will continue to fall for everything we hear and anybody we see. Men cannot love us without loving the almighty GOD first, ladies it is impossible! If you are wondering why you keep getting in bad relationships or marriages this is the reason why, so when you do decide to stop and do it the right way your entire life will change. Stop letting men play with you and not giving you anything except a child or children to raise by yourself. What type of love is it, that you have to raise the child all by yourself, and he doesn't even think you deserve a simple child support check, (which is nothing compared to what it takes to raise a child on your own, all by yourself). Ladies pay attention to the red flags that these guys are wearing on their forehead, they don't even know what they want so how can they be of any assistance to us. Being single allows you to make good sober minded decisions and think things through thoroughly without your mind being overwhelmed with unnecessary confusion that men bring into our life when they don't know what they want. If you are in a relationship or marriage and he has taken away the beautiful smile that GOD has given you, you are in the wrong place; search your heart and follow it. Life is short and we only get one trip on this journey so we might as well make it enjoyable. We get the opportunity to chose, although we sometimes do not prepare ourselves for the consequences and setbacks that come with our decisions, but no one made us make them. We made them because it was what we thought we wanted at the time!

When you become single for whatever the reason might be, accept it, there is a reason that GOD wants you to be single at that particular time in your life. It is not wise to jump into another relationship just to say you are dating because you are not even aware of who you are or what part of you you are willing to share when you're jumping from relationship to relationship. This is how we get wounded, misused, mistreated and hurt; the list could go on and on. Men know when we are hurt and most of them play on that knowing that they don't want to really be with us anyway; they are actually pouring salt on open wounds. They cannot do this to us unless we continue to allow them the opportunity to do so. So why do we do it ladies? We have to say no to more than just drugs! Not saying no is the reason a lot of us have more children than we can take care of. Having and raising children is the hardest job on earth and there is no book to help you in doing it. It doesn't matter what type of college degree you have because every child is and will be different and in most cases you will have to raise them alone. Which means what works for one might not work for the other. If you are continually having children thinking that this is going to keep him, something is entirely wrong with you. It doesn't take three, four, five children to realize that you are with the wrong person and more than likely you are raising them by yourself even though he is with you, so you might as well be by yourself. Many of us have had nervous breakdowns, trips to mental institutions or even are on medications all because we wanted him and he didn't want us. Yes, men can be addictive, just like a drug. You feel you have to have him and no one else will do, you get caught up with him, ladies you all know exactly what I mean.

We as women have to look at the part that we have played in these unfit, unhealthy relationships. Some of these relationships have taken many of us out of the world, just because we wanted to love someone and be loved by someone who didn't love us or could care less about our feelings. We are aware that everyone does not get to share their story but if they do, it is a blessing from GOD. Ladies if you have children and you meet someone that doesn't even have a job, you've got to ask yourself what does he want from you! It doesn't matter how good he looks because looks will not keep the roof over your family's head. We have got to stop settling for less and this is exactly what we have been doing. Many of us are continually doing it at all ages, old and young. Looking for love in all the wrong places, and ending up with men that don't even love themselves. Why? is the million dollar question. Why are we letting these half-grown mean cheat us out of a beautiful life that GOD has already promised us? What is it? It is not just the young women, it is older women as well. When did we lose respect for ourselves? When it comes to men some women are addicted just like a drug they've got to have no matter what he does to them; they need him, they will even run the streets all night looking for him, knowing he is with someone else. He only comes through the back door and not the front door, exactly what does that tell you! If we don't have respect for ourselves these men are not going to respect us. By the time anyone has reached a certain age they have to realize that nothing is new so why are some women that have already lived to be more than half a hundred still settling for nothing when it comes to men? All the games in the book have been played on them and they are still looking for something new. What is it? These are the women that are setting examples and they don't even realize it.

Ladies we have to know that there a two types of men. First of all please don't get it twisted, we do have real men left in the world, it is just sad many of us have not experience having one yet, even including me. Real men does not have the heart to misuse women and leave her standing alone raising his children all by herself. Real men will not accept a woman trying to take care of him because that is not his character, he was not raised like that. Real men have been raised and taught by real men. Second, we have the half-grown men that will never have nothing in life but a story to tell how they went from bed to bed and misused countless numbers of women; most of these men will never get married and will die alone. By the time they have lived to be more than half a hundred, they are starting looking around wondering why they have never been married. Some even have the nerve to call some of us women crazy! Some have children that they might know of and might not and they are not willing to do anything for us but take us to bed and move on to the next woman. We will never get anything from these type of men but heartaches and headaches and most of them want us to take care of them in some kind of way. These are not real men; ladies wake up! If you are dealing with men and all they want to do is drink and party, guess what? All they want from you is sex, everyone in their right mind knows what comes with drinking, drugging, and partying; leave the zero alone and wait for the hero. These are the type of men that are hiding behind something; just let them go on because they have to come to themselves, we can't do it for them. These are the type of men that will make you lose your mind, then they will gladly move on to the next woman and swear up and down that you were already crazy when they met you. Most of us have children so why add another child to your household to raise, it will never work. You cannot raise a grown man, that was apparently his mother's job, and for some reason if she didn't do it, guess what, neither can you!

After being single for six years and doing some research and observing on my own—because we all know that nothing is new under the sun—I can truly see why some women are so jealous of each other and angry at the world. Which of course is wrong, but women you have to ask yourself—what part did you play to get in the position and relationship that you are in? Women stop blaming everyone else for your unwise choices and change them, if you can. When you become single you are able to see things clearly from another spectrum and make the connections in life. Most women that are jealous of other women know deep down in their hearts that they have made unwise choices and they are jealous of other women because they feel that it is too late for them to make a change. But if you are still living it is not too late, when you hold jealousy in your heart against someone this makes your situation worse and it will last even longer. Our heart controls a whole lot and most women don't realize it but GOD knows what is in our heart against other women and women know also because it shows in your face and it comes out of your mouth. Ways and actions do not lie. Don't allow yourself to be jealous at the women that have chosen to do things the right way and have gotten good results. Just do what they did and change your life style so you can get some good results. Everyone has a horrible story that they had to conquer to get to the point where they are in their lives today so don't player hate, hate the game.

Life is all about choices and we get the great opportunity in choosing, so if you chose a man that wants nothing but to go to bed with you, don't be mad at the world be mad at yourself, because you chose him which means apparently you don't want nothing either. Ladies stop being jealous of women that you feel are more beautiful than you; beauty is only skin deep and beauty comes from within. By the way, who told you that you were not beautiful! Don't be mad if you don't like the way GOD has created you and you walk around jealous at every women that you think is more attractive than you are. Take that up with GOD because we didn't have anything to do with how GOD made and created us, but GOD knew who could accept what and who couldn't. Just know that you look the way you look for a reason and just embrace how you look and leave people alone. If it is something that you can change about your appearance, just change, but if not, embrace it, keep going, and move on with your life. We as women spend too much time focusing on things that are irrelevant. It is irrelevant to try and figure out how some women get real men for husbands and some get boys for husbands. Just ask yourself what role did you play, and did you follow GOD's guidelines. If you know you didn't follow GOD's guidelines then why are you mad at other women that did; just do what they did and maybe you will get good results.

When you are single you get the opportunity to realize and know how beautiful and wonderful you are inside and out. You also realized that many things that happen in your life came from your own unwise choices. Being single gives you the opportunity to embrace yourself, know your value and worth, and strive for your highest potential. You can truly enjoy you when you are single; you are aware of your likes and dislikes, you know what you have no intentions of dealing with from other people, and you know what you don't want from men. Being single is an opportunity to learn yourself, love yourself, and be free. Freedom is an opportunity to get on the right track if you are not and an opportunity to follow your own dreams and not live in someone else's nightmare. I have learned to live on nobody's promises but GOD's because all of the rest has and will fail. Being single gives you more opportunities to spend time with GOD so take advantage of it and enjoy your quiet time. Always keep the focus on GOD and you can't go wrong; we were taught right from wrong — do the right thing because it is the right thing to do. Use your own mind; don't let people tell you what they would do if they were you, because it was never meant for them to be you. They don't even know what they should do, so stop taking advice from just anyone because if they are not following GOD who are they following? There is only one choice left. So be careful who you get your advice from; a lot of times the devil is the person giving you the advice, be careful. If they are not following GOD they are lost; they can't help you anyway, run!

"BEING SINGLE IS A BLESSING, NOT A CURSE."

Chapter 2

What Does He Really Want?

You have entered into a relationship with someone that you feel is really right for you. He goes to work every day and visits you frequently and even appears to be somewhat normal. He's aware that you have expenses because he lives on his own so therefore he has expenses as well, but he sees that you have children and that you're trying to make it but he doesn't ever offer you a dime. Why is he showing up at your doorstep every week and never offering or giving you any type of support? He can see that you are struggling because he is struggling, so what does he want with you? This is the number one question we as women have ask ourselves before we decide to allow men to visit and pretend that they want to be a part of our life. If he has nothing to add or contribute to what you already have, what exactly does he want from you? He knew when he met you that you had kids, which means he knows this will be a package deal. You go to work every day, you pay all your bills, and maybe even go to school but this guy can't offer you anything. He probably even wastes hours of your precious time talking on the phone about everything but a committed relationship. What does he really want from you? Does he ask, how was your day? or can I do anything to help you and your kids out? or just give you some cash he knows you need because he does too? So what does he really want from you? On top of that, he is stupid enough to think that you really like him and misses him too but what has he done for you to like him or even miss him?

These are the type of men that will block your doorway and never give you a dime but want to take you out to clubs and buy you drinks all night with the hope that you will get drunk and end up in bed with them. The very next day they have another victim on the list and you have fallen for the game once again and gotten nothing in return but a spirit that you have to live with for the next few months in the hope that he calls you again. What a mess! He goes on about his business and no longer calls or calls whenever he feels like it and has nothing else to do. Now he is running the same game with someone else that he has met and it becomes a cycle for men that don't want anything but sex. How can he possibly think that women can't see through this old game that he is trying to play on them? In the end he will only be playing himself. Ladies why are we wasting our time with men that live with their mother and don't have anything of their own? What does he want from you? He doesn't have anything of his own but he works everyday and still can't offer you anything, so what does he want from you! This is the question that we have to ask ourselves about every man that says he is interested in us. Especially if he doesn't have a job, what do you even want with him? If he doesn't have what you already have, this will be a total setback for you and there is no need to put yourself in that awful situation because it will not work out. You will become frustrated and might even end up losing every-thing that you've accomplished on your own, and guess what—he is ready to move on now and has the nerve to tell everyone that you were crazy!

Ladies have you ever wondered why men that don't have their own place, their own car, or a job would dare to try to get with you? He doesn't have anything to offer, so why waste your time listen-ing to an empty wagon going nowhere? Are we falling for men like this because we are so desperate and don't want to be alone? What is it? What ever happened to our moral values? This is the reason men treat us so badly. Some men are used to many women that don't want anything but a night out and sex, so they apparently think all of us operate the same way. But men please don't get it twisted! We all do not operate the same way. Most men act as if they don't have any morals as well, what type of man will just want to continually go to bed with a woman and do absolutely nothing for her? What type of man is that, and why are we as women allowing that to happen to us? Men can only do what we allow them to do, so wake up women, and stop it. You are worth more than you are getting; you have to know this. Some men do not care who they lie down with, but it doesn't make it okay. How can a man sleep at night knowing that he is not treating her right nor doing anything for this woman but trying to use her? We as women have to ask ourselves: Are we worth more than we have been getting? And until we decide to stand our ground, we will continue to be used and mistreated by men.

Are men actually looking for wives or just so-called friends with benefits? It seems as though everyone wants something for nothing, not realizing that nothing is free. Everything that has ever come easy or free can take a whole lifetime to deal with the consequences, which means more than likely it was not worth it anyway. Ladies when we come into contact with men that don't know where their kids are, that means he is not taking care of them. If you choose to have children with him he is not going to take care of them either. There are so many visible signs that men give us, so why do we still fall in their rat traps, or do we truly miss the signs? If a man comes to you and tells you that he is married but has been separated for many years, run from him! There has to be a very good hidden reason why he doesn't want to divorce his wife that he claims that he doesn't even want. Many relationships and marriages end in separation or divorce, could this be because they were together for the wrong reason or the person was not who they thought they were? This is how so many women have gotten messed up mentally — not realizing that there was nothing they did, but that the person that they were with had the problem. Everyone walks around with excess baggage just waiting to dump it on the next person that they meet. For this reason, when GOD has called us out to be single, we need to embrace it because this gives those open wounds time to heal. If the wounds are not healed the drama will continue, and no matter how hard we try, we will continue to get hurt. Take your time and enjoy the moment wherever you might be in your life, but if you have allowed a man to change who you are then this is not a good relationship. Find your way out before you become bitter at the whole world for your unwise decisions of staying in a messed up marriage or relationship that was never meant to be. Not to mention he probably was somebody else's in the beginning, so who really got fooled?

It is time to stop allowing men to walk over us, because the longer we accept it the longer they will do it. Always keep in mind there are two kinds of men, so you know I am referring to the half-grown men not the real men. Most men don't know what they want just as most women don't really know what they want to a certain degree. In the process everyone is just hurting everyone and continuing on with their life after they have messed up someone else's life. They are walking around with open wounds and allowing people to continue to throw salt on them. Everyone is moving from person to person and trying to change people, which was never our job in the first place. This is and always will be GOD's job and some of us have spent a lifetime trying to change people and have messed our entire life up trying to do GOD's job. Another example of an angry woman, mad because she can't change her man, not realizing that it was never her job in the first place. Now she walks around with madness in her heart and every time she sees someone that appears to be happy and have it all together she gets jealous — why is that! This is the main reason most people don't become successful in life; they have too much hatred in their heart for no reason at all, not realizing that they are the ones that made those choices. Which means they are the ones that have to deal with and live through the consequences, so don't be mad at other people for your choices.

When we as women come to the conclusion and realize that we are our own biggest problem, maybe some of us might be willing to change our unattractive attitude toward people. I have worked with the public the majority of my life and I never saw so many angry women — angry because they are not happy at home. They have made unwise choices and think that it is too late to change, but in the meantime they are holding jealousy, envy, and strife in their hearts and this is what cuts their blessing from GOD. Many people don't realize that no one can cut your blessing but you; it is not the other person, it is you and only you. Most of the time women are jealous of other women because they admire them but don't have enough courage to tell them that. On the other hand they play the phony friends games which people can see straight through. God gave us enough wisdom and knowledge to know when people are jealous of us and don't like us, so stop faking, women. Stand up and own up to the choices that you have made and if you don't want to live with the consequences, move on; don't player hate on other females, they didn't have anything to do with the choices that you made. The world cannot help it if he does not want you, it is not our fault. What role did you play to get in that unfit relationship? Ladies keep in mind that true love does not hurt, so if you are in a relationship or marriage and are getting hurt over and over again, there is a huge problem. What is it? Only you can answer that question.

"DOES HE WANT <u>YOU</u> OR WHAT YOU <u>HAVE</u>?"

Chapter 3

Do You Really Love Yourself?

Why are there so many women that dress their men, make sure they are well groomed, send them to the barbershop, etc., and don't do anything for themselves? They don't seem to realize that they are grooming and dressing him for someone else. Again, what type of man will accept this—and you are walking around looking like Raggedy Ann. We are queens, which means we should look our best at all times. We are the prize, don't let those men fool you like they are the prize because they are not. If a man can never compliment you or tell you how beautiful you are, what is he good for, because these are some of the simple things, and most men fail at the simple things. Very few still open the door as you approach a building, not to mention getting into and out of a car. They will drive off before you close the door nowadays. What ever happened to the real role models, all of them can't be dead! But remember there a two types of men and we know which category this one fits into. A lot of men don't even remember your birthday women, so what does that tell you. I have to admit real men do recognize beautiful and real women, it is the half-grown men that don't. Ladies, if we really love ourselves we are not going to settle for just anything or anybody; we have to have set standards for ourselves; we have to require and expect more for ourselves.

If you know you want to be married, don't waste your time with these guys that are just out for what they can get, because they will never have nothing and they don't want you to have anything. If they all telling you all they want is to be friends, run from them; they want friends with benefits. Most of the men that are not considering marriage just want to take you to the club and back home, usually your place and not his. Leave those type of men alone, trust me when I say they are sick and don't even know it. They can care less about your last name, but they can only do this if we allow them to. Which means ladies, you have the upper hand, why are you not taking it? Ladies, why are you expecting men to respect you when you don't even respect yourself? If you don't respect yourself they never will respect you. Respect is not automatic: it must be earned. If you don't love yourself, you don't respect yourself, and you will settle for anything or anybody you can get with, on the assumption that you can't do better. This is living in denial. You want better but you don't feel that you deserve better, because you have been brain washed by a man with low self-esteem. He gets a kick out of disrespecting you and treating you any kind of way, like you are going to tolerate that forever. However, this is when he gets fooled because most women — when they get tired of being tired — they do learn and do better. The women that are not trying to do better, they haven't learnt yet and they are not tired of being tired yet; they are still doing the same thing looking for different results and we all know what that means. They are continually starting over in different relationships and nothing is changing but his name, face, and address — but until they get tired of being tired, they will continue to do the same thing and blame everyone but themselves. This is another example of an angry woman mad at the world because she can't get it right and chose not to try, but in the meantime she envies every woman she comes in contact with because it appears to her that the other woman have it all together. Therefore, this leaves envy, jealously, and strife in her heart and now she will never get it right because GOD judges our heart — not what we say or do. Our mouth will say one thing but our heart shows the real deal, and GOD knows and sees what is really within our heart.

Sometimes we have to take a step back and search our hearts, because this could be the reason why we go through some of what we go through. Search your heart; the heart don't lie. It is okay to ask yourself why you are jealous of a certain person because only you can answer that question. Especially, if you know this person has done absolutely nothing to you. Women, why would you be jealous because your man looks at a beautiful woman when she pass him by, this is what he's supposed to do, besides why are you jealous of the woman, when your man did the looking? He can look but that doesn't mean he has to touch her; this could be telling you to get yourself together because you are beautiful as well, you just have to bring it out sometimes. We all are beautiful but some of our ways are not. We also have to remember that beauty is only skin deep. It is what's behind the beauty that is really going to count in the end. Ladies, if we truly loved ourselves there is no way we would do some of the things that we do. Until we love ourselves no one is going to love us, they are just going to continue to use us and get whatever it is they want out of us. The average person doesn't even know the meaning of love. Love is a word that people just use to get what they want out of you. Love is an action word, how can a man open his mouth and say he loves you and he isn't doing anything for you but using you? How did this get to be love? What kind of love is he referring too; he doesn't know you and he doesn't know what love is. Love is just a word that men use to get what they want, when they want it, and guess what—you probably aren't the only women that he is saying that to. You're struggling, paying all the bills, working just like he is working and taking care of your kids, and he can't offer you any type of help— but he loves you. Now that I really can't and don't understand! Why are we accepting this from men, are we that desperate that we have to settle for nothing just so we will not be alone? No you don't have to settle for nothing unless you choose too; the choice is yours. You get what you except, if you except nothing he is not going to give you anything. Now when it comes to real men, there is no way in the world they are going to accept a woman taking care of them. It takes their manhood away, a man is supposed to take care of his wife and family, and only real men do that. Real men are consistent in the things that they do. They don't say one thing and do something entirely different. Thank GOD we still have some of them left on earth. Ladies, we don't realize how we handicap men, after handicapping them then they move on and they look for the same thing from every woman they meet. If a man gets use to a woman taking care of him he is going to look for that in every woman he meets. This makes it hard for the real women, because we are not use to taking care of men, especially if we have children; we are used to men contributing to the family. This is how society is messed up. Ladies, if you are among the women that do take care of their men, you need to reevaluate yourself. There is no way you can truly love yourself and accept this. Whoever told you this was okay, they misinformed you. Somewhere down the line you missed a whole lot because this is not the norm. Ladies do it because they think it is okay and they think this will keep him but it is not and it will not keep him if he really wants to go. He will never become a man as long as you are taking care of him, and treating him like a child. That was his mother job's, and if his own mother got tired of him, what on earth do you think is going to happen to you?

"He that finds a wife, finds a good thing." Ladies if you are taking care of him, nine times out of ten you found him and that is the problem. Real men find us, we don't find them. This is the reason the divorce rate is higher than ever and still rising, even in the Christian homes. Many of us have married for the wrong reasons and once we said I do, he was everything that we didn't dream of, and he wants us to play the role of his mother. If we truly want peace and happiness that GOD has promised up, we have to set standards for ourselves and learn to do it GOD's way. This is the only way you are going to get both peace and happiness here on earth. If you have not learned and followed GOD's guidelines you are going to continue to go through unnecessary drama that could have been avoided. You can pray all day and all night long but if you do not follow GOD guidelines it is going to be a big mess — but GOD will keep you in your right mind to deal with the mess you created. Ladies, stop getting these men that have never experienced living on their own and having responsibilities of their own; you already know most of them probably have never taken care of anything but stray dogs, so what does that tell you! Ladies, there has to be a reason GOD left us guidelines to follow; did you ever stop and think why GOD did that? There has to be a healthy and beneficial reason why. He knew we didn't have sense enough to choose a soul mate, because GOD is the only one that can truly see what is deep down in a person's heart. We are looking at the surface and listening to what they say but marriage goes deeper than the surface and what we see; this is the reason we keep messing it up. Have you ever wondered how everything was going so good until you decided to get married? That's because you were doing things that you should not have been doing until you were married, and now you have messed up everything and are left trying to fix it yourself. It is GOD's job to fix things; fixing things was never our job because GOD knew we didn't have enough sense to fix things on our own. This is the reason he is GOD and we need him and must follow his guidelines.

We spend a whole lifetime trying to change people without realizing that we are the ones that need to change, because GOD never gave us the power nor permission to change anyone. We stress ourselves out for years, but all the time we also notice that nobody is changing but us. We are stressed out and he is living his life and having fun. We sit and worry about things that we cannot change all the time, but why is it so hard for us to realize that we can't change anyone? We spend too much time and energy worrying about things that really don't matter. Everyone is always trying to find an easier way to do what is right, but there is nothing easy about doing what is right. If it was all that easy, society would not be the way it is today. There are no short cuts to life; if you take the short cuts you will have to redo almost everything – so why not just do the right thing because it is right? If things are happening easy for you in your life this simply means you are doing something wrong. It was never written in any book that things were going to be easy. If it came to you easy you will have to deal with the consequence almost the rest of your entire life. Don't look for easy ways out by accepting anything that comes your way, because every time you settle for less, it is a setback in your life and more than likely you will at some point have to start all over again and nobody is worth you starting all over again and again. The more and more we have to start over the longer our process is going to be, we have to get to a point in our lives when we ask ourselves, "Is this man worth me starting over?" Let me answer that for you right now. No he is not worth you start over because if he was worth it you would not have to start over, so wake up! We don't get younger we only get older, so why spend half your life unhappy because of bad choices? It was a choice and GOD gives us all choices, so when you continue to make unwise choices over and over again don't be mad at the world because you need to be delivered.

"LEARN TO LOVE YOURSELF FIRST!

YOU HAVE TO SAY NO TO MORE THAN DRUGS."

Chapter 4

How to Get On The Right Track

Well, first of all, if you are living together and are not married, throw him out. Shacking up is a not a very good choice. Why? Because if he gets to play house with you more than likely he will not want to marry you. For example, it is just like test driving a car, if you get to test drive it for a while you then realize that you really don't like it the way you thought you did and now you no longer care for or have interest in it. Why give a man the pleasure of trying you out to be his wife, because more than likely you will not be the one he wants to spend the rest of his life with. Stop telling everyone he is your fiancé; he has been your fiancé for many years and all you have is a house full of kids with broken promises and no type of ring on your finger. He is not your fiancé, he is your financial problem because when he gets tired of you, financial problems are exactly what you are going to have trying to raise his kids all by yourself is. Don't be fooled; we all can use those lines. We need to get to know a person, but you will never really know a person. Why do you think people are still getting divorces after twenty and thirty years of marriage? Wake up! What is it you need to know? He has done everything but marry you; it is what it is. He either wants you or he doesn't; don't be a fool all your life. You have cheated yourself and don't even realize it, and it doesn't matter how many children you have had, he is not obligated to marry you and probably won't.

If you are single, it is okay to live a celibate life, that doesn't mean anything is wrong with you. It only mean you have set standards and until a real man finds you, you choose to follow GOD's standards. Besides, you have already tried everything else and it didn't work, so what do you really have to lose? Nothing is new, the game is old; we meet the same type of people with different names. The game doesn't change; we know the game. Stop acting desperate, like you have never had a man and keep falling for the first thing that comes across your path. If we stand up, trust me, he will stand up. I truly believe we can do bad all by ourselves without a man breathing down our back every night and not satisfying us in no kind of way! Stop cheating yourself, women! It is time to stop making things so easy for these men; this is the reason they don't know how to be real men. Some of us, we have to admit, we bring it on ourselves and that makes it our fault. We as women have to take the setbacks, because if kids are involved there will be a lot of things in life we will have to wait and put on hold. For some reason the women always end up with the hardest job: raising the kids.

The longer we continue to let this happen, the more they will continue to do it to us and think nothing of it. He doesn't care if you have one, two, three, or even four babies if he doesn't want you, he is not going to stay with you. So who has to suffer? We see this everyday but yet we continue to lie down with them and fall into the same traps over and over again and continue to have their babies. What we don't realize and understand is, half-grown men don't know what **to** do with babies. So how many years of your life do you want to continue not getting sleep, getting up throughout the night preparing baby bottles, and not to mention what comes along with them actually growing up—the choices are all ours. This is the reason they will make babies so fast, because they don't know and don't have the responsibility of taking care of them; they feel that it is your responsibility all by yourself because they have moved on to someone else. But this is the same person who claimed he loved you so much and couldn't do without you and now he wants to act as if you are the worst woman on earth. Some will even drag your name in the mud. But what men don't realize is, we are still the mother of their children, so what does that make them if we are so bad and awful? After the two of you go your separate ways he wants to play Santa Claus in the kids' life and he really thinks this is being a real father.

But why do they do us like that? Because we allow them to, over and over again — with the hope that the outcome will be different the next time around. We think jumping and getting married is the solution to the problem or even getting pregnant, but this only brings hatred into your heart because you knew he didn't really want you and wasn't going to treat you right anyway. Then we wonder why we can't get along with each other anymore. It was never really meant for us to get along, it was suppose to be a one night out event, but that's all it takes to change your whole life and your goals. When we jump and marry just because we are pregnant that is not owning up to responsibilities, that is creating an endless mess, because more than likely you will be in divorce court and then he forgets his responsibilities until the judge has to remind and demand him of them. This is so sad but it is true and most of the children have to suffer because of the confused parents making unwise choices; and we have the nerve to wonder what is wrong with our kids. Our kids are confused; they don't know what to think or how to think, because the parents are saying one thing and doing the opposite. But if we expect for our kids to act right, how is this going to happen if they don't know how? Because most of us don't know how. We get first hand with our own children in most cases, so whatever they see us do they are going to try it at some point in their life. It is going to be in the back of their mind: mom and dad use to do it so it must be okay. We are role models for our kids, but are we actually setting good examples? We can't blame this situation on anyone but us. This is always the question; what kind of influence have you had over your child's life?

Until we stand up and do what is right because it is right nothing will change. We will have spent our entire life talking about what we should have done and in the meantime everything remains the same. Everyone realizes that this is not a perfect world and we are going to make unwise choices and mistakes in life but at what point do we learn from the mistakes that we have made? If we keep doing the same thing over and over and looking for different results we can't call anyone crazy but ourselves. GOD give us all choices, he doesn't demand or force us to do anything, so what is the problem ladies? We are our own worst enemy and we don't even realize it, but we want to put the blame on everyone else but ourselves. This is not right at all. Whether our mother, father, grandma, etc. raised us, someone taught us right from wrong; we know that if it is not right it has to be wrong, there is no in between. So why is it so hard to determine what is right? Why are we accepting these men that will not do anything for us but take us to bed? There is something wrong with them, but guess what—something is wrong with us too.

Until we do what is right because it is right we will never get on the right track. We will forever be used by men and live our lives angry at everyone else because we chose to have nothing in life and everyone else wanted more. Now you are walking around with an unrealistic attitude that all men are the same, which is not true! Ladies, please don't let the devil fool you like that. All men are not the same, we just have two different categories of men, the ones who want something and the ones who don't, just like the women, that is the only difference. Ask yourself which category do you fit in; only you can answer that question and it doesn't take you very long to figure it out, just look around you. Ladies, we deserve so much better. GOD has promised us peace and happiness, but for some reason the majority of the women are not happy and this is because they are trying to do it on their own. Trying to do what on their own? They are trying to find their own soul mate and this is not the way that GOD wants us to do it. How many men do we have to go through and how many innocent babies do we have to bring into the world to figure out we don't know what we are doing, the job is much too hard for us. This is the reason GOD gave us the guidelines, and they do work, but you will never know that they work until you try them. It is not too late, you just have to make up your mind that you are not going to settle for less anymore and just do it. There is never nothing to it but to do it, and no one can stop you but you. When we as women take the time to realize that we are the only one that is stopping ourselves, we will do something about it.

Some of us have come to that realization, but so many are still in denial and looking for someone else to blame and point the finger at. In the meantime, we are not getting anywhere in life, and we are cheating ourselves, and we can't blame anyone but ourself. When we begin to want more for ourselves and our kids we will no longer settle for a half-grown man that wants nothing but our flesh. We will continue to accept men that don't want anything out of life but sex, but until we get tired of being tired we will continue our journey doing the same thing, looking for different results. The best way to get on the right track is to do what is right because it is right, and please don't do to anyone what you do not want done to you.

"SUBMIT YOUR LIFE TO CHRIST AND DO WHAT IS RIGHT
BECAUSE IT IS RIGHT!"

Chapter 5

Why Are Most Women So Angry?

Most women are angry because they know that they have cheated themselves for the majority of their lives. Most women didn't follow GOD's guidelines and this is the end result, a bad marriage or bad relationship. It doesn't matter how old you are or how long you've been married. If you did not do it the way GOD has asked us to do it, you have been living a nightmare and you are still asleep because you are in denial. It doesn't matter if they are eighty years old or fifteen years old. Many women have been in long time marriages for twenty, thirty, forty years or more and have been miserable the entire time — and now they hold hatred in their hearts toward every woman who looks happy. Many have had several children thinking that was going to stop him from cheating, but instead they had to stay home and keep the children while he took the opportunity to do and see whoever he wanted — and they are mad behind that. Many women have broken up marriages and taken other women's spouses only to realize that he wasn't what she thought he was, and now they are angry — because she no longer wants him and he surely doesn't want her. She is angry because he is now cheating on her and now she is getting her payback. Many women have set traps for their so-called friends and have fallen into them themselves and they are angry. Many have been in long relationships and marriages and they know that they have not been the only one the entire time, and they are angry about that. Many have dealt with long time spouses who have created another entire family, and they are angry about that. Many have gotten into the marriage for the wrong reason and now it doesn't work and nobody loves each other anymore, and they are angry about that. Many spent years sneaking around with this man and when they finally got together and got married they realized he really didn't want them, and they are angry about that.

These are examples why many women are so jealous and angry at the world and other women. But guess what? This is what they chose, so don't be mad at other people; take a look in the mirror and blame yourself. Everyone deep down inside knows how they got into their relationship, and if by any chance he was married and was somebody else's when you met, you have cursed yourself for life; it is called payback. So don't even wonder why he doesn't want you and isn't treating you right. This is the unnecessary drama that we get on our journey of life when we decide to not do it GOD's way. Being in an unfit relationship or marriage can one of be the worst experiences ever, while traveling on our journey, because if you live through it you have to give GOD the glory. There is no easy way, there is only one right way, which is GOD's way or it will not work. Who wants to be married and living in separate rooms from their spouse, not even sleeping in the same bed; this is not a marriage this is a mess.

And this is why many women, especially the older ones, are angry, and never have a smile on their face. They have spent over half their life in a marriage and can't even stand to look their man in the eye, not to mention kiss him. Now she is angry at everyone because she is no longer a size five, seven or even nine or she is no longer beautiful as she thought she was, and now her spouse is noticing everyone but her. More than likely he was somebody else's man when she met and married him and this is the end result! Payback! What goes around does come back around. Ladies, ask yourself; who's spouse did you take? Are you now stuck with someone else's drama and nightmares? Leave other women's husbands alone unless you are ready to live with the dead end consequences. This is why she is angry.

If we as young women have to follow GOD's guidelines, this means that when the older women were younger, they were suppose to follow those same guidelines as well, because GOD's word does not change, and everyone that reads the Bible knows this. So why are you so angry? This is the reason people are unhappy in their marriage, and they know this deep down inside — especially if they know GOD. The older women sit back and criticize the young women because they are doing the same thing that they have done and use to do. Instead they should be advising them and trying to talk to them, instead of criticizing them. How can you criticize someone when you know deep down inside you did the same thing? Some women are angry because they don't look the way they want to look or maybe used to look, so they are angry and jealous of other women. Not realizing that GOD created everyone to look the way that they look, this should be something that they should take up with GOD and not out on other people. If there happens to be something about you that you can change, then change it, — if not, don't worry about it. True beauty comes from within and the more anger you show toward people the uglier you look inside and out, check yourself, ladies!

GOD has allowed us to see couples that have done it GOD's way; we can see the glow all around them, and they are not angry at anyone. So this lets us know that it can be done because there are people that have done it — couples who have never heard of the madness that women had to go through who didn't wait on GOD. There is a difference. If you don't think so you better ask somebody or read the Bible for yourself. Who wants just to live a miserable life and then die? Life is supposed to have at least some peace and happiness; how many people do you know that have that peace and happiness in their marriage? Probably very few. Trust me, it does exist, but you have to do it GOD's way in order to experience it. Until you make up in your mind to do it the right way you will spend the rest of your life miserable, mean, and mad. But you can only be mad at yourself, because only you know how you got into the marriage or relationship that you are in, and why you are still there, angry and unhappy. Ladies, take a good look in the mirror and who do you see, staring back at you? Nothing will change until you change. Stop walking around angry at everyone for the choices you made. Nothing is worse than going in the store and the cashier is angry at the customers while taking their money, not realizing that without customers he or she couldn't be a cashier. Take those frustrations and turn them around into something positive,. Yes, I agree that life might not be always fair, but GOD is fair because we reap the seeds that we sow, it doesn't get any better than that. So if your life has been on the wrong track all your life, it is time to examine yourself and search your heart, because something is not adding up. GOD is good to everybody. He also judges us by what is in our heart. Nothing is worse than a person telling you how happy they are for you, but you can see nothing but jealousy all in their eyes. Who do they think they are fooling? Not GOD; only themselves. For some people, the contents of their hearts has been a setback for many years. We are holding bitterness in our hearts because we think somebody owes us something, but they don't. If there is anything you want in life that is worth something you are going to have to make the sacrifices to accomplish it. No one is going to give you anything but bad advice, and we can't live on no one's promises but GOD's. So what that he cheated on you and left you, so what you didn't get the job you thought you were going to get, so what she looks better than you, so what you are broke—who cares? The list can go on and on, but what makes you any different from anyone else? Life goes on and we will live with you or without you, it doesn't matter except to you.

Don't make other people pay for your mistakes, it not fair because you have a choice in every decision that you make because GOD gave us a choice. If you are unhappy and angry at the world this is your problem and you just need to be delivered from all that evil that is down in your heart, then you can have peace and happiness here on earth. One thing about life is when we make our bed we will have to lie in it, so what part did you play in making your own bed that you are now lying in and it hurt so bad and now you are angry at everyone. Being a woman is coming to grips with the unwise choices that you have made and owning up to them and not blaming everyone else but yourself. Being a woman is rising up being yourself, trusting and believing in GOD, stop putting your trust in people and depending on them and keep on moving in the right direction. Always look at yourself first, before you try and blame someone else, we as women are our biggest problem and we can't even see it because we are so busy focusing on someone else instead of ourselves.

Life is what you make out of it, if you want nothing, you get nothing. If you want something out of life you can get it, but no one is going to hand it to you, and if you have not lived long enough to figure this out just keep on living and you will see who is truly on your side. GOD already knew we weren't capable of making sound decisions for ourselves; this is the reason he promised to never leave us alone. Every time we jump out in front of GOD, trying to do things on our own, we mess it up and have the nerve to wonder why it didn't work. There is no way around GOD's way and I am sure everyone at some point has tried it but ask yourself, did it work? We've spent a lot of years repeating and starting over, doing the same thing over and over again looking for new results; this is not how it was meant to be. We women bring most of these unnecessary changes on ourselves. Every time we have to start over it is a setback in our life and this makes the process even longer and harder for us, and we have the nerve to wonder why it takes so much work to get ahead. Ask yourself what part you played. Own up to it and move on; we are entitled to mistakes — no one is perfect. But don't use this as an excuse to continue doing the same thing over and over and over again, because it doesn't work like that. You are only fooling yourself. The whole world already knows the real story; there are no secrets in life and nothing is hidden or covered up, so you are not fooling anyone but yourself. All we have to do is keep living and GOD shows us everything; this is the reason we don't have to worry about anything or anybody because GOD will show us what we need to see in the time we need to see it. GOD will also show us how people really are and what they really think about us.

Don't ever think that there is no way out; there is always a way out of your situation. You just have to take it when the opportunity is presented to you. Ladies, this is where we mess up, thinking that we have to accept anything that comes our way, but it's not true. Remember, GOD gave us all choices, we just have to make the best choice for us and nobody knows that better than us. Don't waste your time and energy listening to people that don't even know what they want out of life because they are going to make sure we are just as confused as they are, and remain where they are. Forget about so-called friends; they only want what you have, especially if you are married and they are not—leave them alone. Most women have been betrayed the most by their so-called friends, and that is a wound that takes a long time to heal; it can take longer than being hurt by your own spouse. Ladies, stop letting women get close to you like that—talking on the phone all the time, what do they want? Talking about my friend, we don't have friends, they just want to be nosy and that's it. These type of women will be jealous of you the most, the ones that you talk on the phone with from day to day, so stop it, it is irrelevant and a waste of your time. Women that talk on the phone all the time do not have a life and don't have anything else to do. All you have to do is take a look at their life—it speaks for itself. Most of the time the person on the other end of the telephone is either the devil or one of his workers, so be careful; they don't want anything, and can care less about you or what you do. Please don't be fooled by the devil. GOD shows us what we need to see; when GOD shows us, please believe him. Once we find them out they know it, because they will no longer call you because the devil doesn't like being revealed. After spending hours and hours on the telephone month after month and all the time the devil was on the other end, what a disappointment, but life goes on. For some reason it ends up like that with every female you meet. Have you ever asked yourself why this is? It is because they are jealous of you and admire you and don't know how to tell you. Yes, it is that simple, and we call ourselves women. Real women can tell the truth and not have jealousy and hatred in their hearts and eyes against you, and they will truly be happy for you. This is what makes women angry; they have envy, jealousy, and strife in their hearts. This is also what cut their blessing, because no one can cut your blessing better than you; only you can do it. Women, if you need to talk to somebody, try talking to GOD; he is the only one you don't have to worry about changing on you or getting jealous of you, and he is not going to tell your business, because he is the same yesterday, today, and forever more. Stay off the phone and go to the throne.

"STOP BLAMING EVERYONE FOR YOUR CHOICES

and

LOOK IN THE MIRROR!"

Chapter 6

Living a Celibate Life

If you have read my autobiography you can understand why I have chosen to live a celibate life. This is one of the best choices that I have made in my life and I am looking forward to the benefits that come with doing it GOD's way. I chose to live a celibate life because I was tired of giving my all and all and getting nothing in return but heartaches and headaches in unhealthy marriages and relationships. I feel that GOD did prepare me to live a celibate lifestyle because it can be challenging at times, but anything that is worth having and making sacrifices toward will be worth more in the end. Besides, what isn't a challenge in life! I do realize that it is nothing that I am doing on my own without GOD. GOD allows me to live a celibate life; I can't do anything on my own. Living a celibate life illuminates all the drama that comes along with unhealthy, unfit relationships.

I have chosen to live a celibate lifestyle because I am preparing myself to become married again someday. Once again it is a choice, one that GOD allowed me to make. I truly believe that GOD was preparing me during my married years to live a celibate life, because being in consistent abusive and unhealthy relationships you are not being loved, you are being misused, abused and played over. This makes it easier for me because I really can't miss anything that I have never had, which is true love and someone who really knows how to treat and respect me the way that women should be treated and respected. Since GOD has already shown me that I don't really have true friends other than him, I don't waste a lot of my time on the telephone, I try to spend as much quiet time with GOD as I can. I take advantage of my precious, value time, because our time is valuable and we have to make it all count toward something positive or we might end up losing out on many things in life. Always remember, we only get one life to live and it is up to each individual however they choose to live it. For I do realize that I am still on my real life journey and I do have to admit it has been a lonely one all by myself, but I know it is going to be well worth the walk in the end. One thing about life is, when you decide to live for Jesus and only Jesus, he will show you everyone that is against you. Yes, it hurts sometimes, but what can I say. Life goes on with or without them and more than likely they weren't supposed to be in your life anyway.

I spent many years being nice to people and trying to give them good advice, trying to help them get through obstacles that I had already been through and telling them how good GOD is and the things that GOD had done in my life — and those people betrayed me. I have to believe that it was all in GOD's plan because when we are walking with GOD he does direct our path. When people come into your life, GOD has to let you know what they are about, because they come in disguise like they really like you and have your best interests at heart — but deep down inside they have an agenda. When things doesn't go the way that they thought they should go then they flip the script on you real fast. And want you to think that it is you when it was them all the time, now they are disappointed because GOD showed them up; the devil hates when he has been revealed. Nothing is worse than going out of your way for a so-called friend, you know you have been nothing but nice to them, you have even done things for them that you knew they would not have done for you, and they have the nerve to flip the script on you. Also have the nerve to be jealous and envious of you too, and they think you can't see through them. Wow! The devil is a liar! That is your positive sign to leave them alone. It is not you, please don't think it is; they have deep serious issues. Don't try to figure it out; just move on and pray for them.

Since my last husband did me the favor of leaving, I decided it was time for me to get it right. So when I get married this one last time, it will be right. Living a celibate and clean sober minded life helps you to see everyone for who they really are and you set your standards for GOD. The sky is the limit; GOD told us we could have whatever we want, all we had to do is ask as long as we are living according to his will. I refused to let a man play with me and I get nothing in return but headaches and heartaches. I spent twenty years of my life doing this and I have come to the conclusion that enough is enough and no one can stop it but me. The old tricks that most men play; they don't work anymore. He has to be bringing something to the table other than a smile on his face and sex. I have chosen to live my life for GOD which means I don't have to accept just anything or anyone anymore, GOD has promised me the best as long as I do it his way and live for him. It have been several years now and yes I do get lonely because I am human, but I get to sleep well at night because I don't have to deal with anyone's drama but mine. Thank GOD!

Since I am totally single and free, I am really enjoying me. I can go to the movies and laugh out loud all by myself; it feels great, I can go out and eat all by myself, etc. and it is truly a great feeling enjoying me. In the meantime I am continually reaching and setting goals for myself, and preparing myself for the husband that GOD is preparing for me. It is not going to be junk, it is going to be the best because only GOD has sense enough to chose the best for us—we don't. The waiting process is what many women don't want to go through, they want real, good men, but they don't want to wait and do it the right way to actually get them. There are things we have to do in order to make that happen, because nothing just happens. If we don't follow GOD's guidelines we will keep getting the same thing and hoping it will turn out different every time, but it won't—and deep down inside we already know it. When we make a change, everything and everyone around us will change. I have a made up mind, I have no intentions of settling for any type of drama that I have already been through in my life, because I don't have too. I know I have choices, and no one can make me believe that I don't anymore. I have truly a lot to look forward to because in my past all I ever got was disappointments, letdowns, setbacks, etc., and I realized that no one could change that but me. I am not angry at anyone nor do I hold any hatred in my heart toward anyone that played a part because that is history now. I am looking for bigger and better things in life. I no longer have to settle and I know this now. The men I had in the past didn't deserve me anyway, it is truly their loss and not mine. I am finally enjoying the peace and happiness that GOD has for us. I no longer have to argue or get upset because of him, there is no him and this is how I get peace and happiness; it is truly amazing how much drama a man can bring into your life and make your life a living hell because he doesn't know what or who he wants and you weren't supposed to be with him anyway. What a waste of time and energy! I thank GOD for showing me the light and delivering me. Now I put all that energy into doing something positive like educating myself, setting goals for myself, and most of all enjoying myself and GOD. I thank GOD everyday for opening my blinded eyes to the world and especially being able to see the half-grown men for exactly who they are and what they really want. For the most part, they don't even come or look my way, it must be written all over my face, "She don't play games," and I am glad about it. No mess, no stress. I am at a point in my life that I would have never dreamed of, but all I can say is, "GOD is good all the time and all the time GOD is good." Always treat people the way you want to be treated and you cannot go wrong. Remember what goes around does come back around when you least expect it too.

In order to realize and know who you are, you have to know yourself; many men don't give us an opportunity to be ourselves. We are so busy trying to please and satisfy him and he doesn't want us anyway, yes it does seem like a waste of time but it also makes us more of a woman if we get out of the relationship before it is too late, before we have completely lost our minds. Now for all the women who wants to submit their life to Christ and live for GOD, this is the best way to live. And the ones that don't want to do it GOD's way, don't player hate when GOD blesses us with real men, just do what we did to get them. Again, this is a choice not a demand; we all make our own choices, but we also have to be prepared to live with the consequences. Jealously is the number one thing that most people struggle with, especially women, they say they are not jealous, but their ways and actions shows us the truth. There is no need to be jealous of anyone because I guarantee you, no one would want to switch journeys with anyone at any given time. So women, search your own hearts and stop trying to judge other women. If you want what they got, just do what they did to get it. Ladies, submitting our life to Christ is the only way to get the best things that GOD has for us. GOD is good to everyone and all he wants is for us to do the right thing — and we can have whatever we want. We don't have to be jealous of one another, because whatever GOD has for us, our name is already on it. And NO one can take it, so relax! We should be embracing one another and helping one another to make it through this journey, because it is not easy, especially for those who have submitted their life to Christ, because the devil wants us back. We need each other to make it on this journey, so encourage one another and show love to one another; this is what GOD wants us to do: help someone else along the way.

When we think about all the years we wasted chasing a cloud of smoke, we have to want so much better for our lives. Besides, only what we do for Christ will last. It is all about saving souls, not about being jealous of one another. There is a judgment day coming and what do you want GOD to say about you on that day? Everyone will have to stand before GOD for themselves and guess what, he's not going to want to hear excuses, so we need to get it right before it is too late. You can't go wrong living for GOD because he is not going to let you go wrong, it is just a matter of having a made up mind. You are either living for GOD or the devil there is no in-between, and only you can answer that. Because you can't live for both.

Ladies, if you are tired of being tired and don't know what to do or where to go, just try GOD. I bet you your life you will not regret it, besides most of you have already tried any and everything else and you have to admit that nothing else has worked. So what are you waiting on, GOD is waiting for you. He never left us, we left him, and GOD will forgive us; all we have to do is surrender — it works. I found out for myself, and I have not regretted it one bit, because I know I am safe in his arms and GOD will never let me down. So what will make you any different from me? In GOD's eyes all of us are the same, there are no little eyes or big eyes, just come as you are. Because if you are waiting to get yourself together on your own, it will never happen, because we don't know how. This is the reason we need GOD, please don't let it be too late because we don't have forever. Life is short, look around you. Living a celibate and sober minded life I am able to observe and see a lot of unnecessary changes that many women are going through when they really don't have to, but some of them really think they do. Young and old, it doesn't matter the age; if you are in a unhealthy, unfit marriage or relationship, it shows all over your face, and in your ways and actions. So I have to assume that you didn't follow the guidelines that GOD left for us to abide by. We all know that life comes with trials and tribulations as do marriages and relationships — but we have to be true to ourselves. We can't act as if GOD has put all this drama together that some women are enduring because GOD is not in any mess. GOD is a GOD of decent order and peace; is peace in your home? Only you can answer that. When GOD puts it together it isn't the same, because if it was, why did he leave us guidelines to follow? This is the big misunderstanding that a lot of women have about marriage, and this is the reason there is so much unnecessary drama in their lives.

What on earth would possibly make you think that you will have a successful relationship or marriage without GOD? This is what we don't realize as women, we jump into relationships and marriages just because they might look good and don't have a clue as to what we are doing. Most of us we know we don't or didn't seek GOD first, we were just in the flesh and we wanted what we wanted at the time. Five, ten, twenty years, etc. later we are very angry at who we are with because he is nothing like we thought and everything has changed and went bad, and everyone is trying to find an easy way out of it, but there is no easy way. The bottom line is, although many women, especially the seasoned women, don't want to admit it, but they already know deep down inside that they didn't wait on GOD and do it his way, and I don't care how old they are. There is no secret, it shows all over their face along with their ways and actions. The rules apply to all, so don't be in denial, it is what it is. Most of you know you didn't wait on GOD or seek GOD before you said "I do"; you did it yourself, and now you are angry at the world because it has been a complete nightmare, and many of you are stuck in it, because where are you going to go at this point and age in your life? Ladies, let's not cheat ourselves like this; everyone can look around and see how we've cheated ourselves like this; it is no secret who wants to live angry at the world once we get older. The choice again is ours. Try to make right decisions and choices, because we truly have to live with the consequences. No one is worth living a life of misery—mean and mad because we don't want to be with them and they don't want to be with us. There is no secret, so who is really fooling who?

**"CHOOSE A CELIBATE LIFE
IF YOU WANT THE REAL MAN THAT YOUR HEART DESIRES!"**

Chapter 7

Why Are Women So Phony?

Most women act phony because they don't like themselves for whatever reason. Some might not be even aware of it. They don't know how to be true to themselves, so it is impossible for them to be true to each other. Women can be evil toward each other, but why is this? Because they are not happy about the choices that they have made. Some of them have allowed life to just pass them by while focusing on things and people that didn't matter anyway. Women meet each under false pretense and act like they want to be your friend, knowing deep down inside they are not happy for you in any kind of way. Most of them don't even know the meaning of friend, you are only a friend if you gossip with them, especially on the telephone or you have something that they are trying to get out of you to use you. But they allow themselves to be nice enough to get out of you what they want, then turn on you and share everything you confided with someone else (and telling them to not tell anyone). This is what phony so-called friends do for you. The game is not new, this is an old game; you'd think the older the women becomes the more mature they would act—not true. Most of the time they are the worst, because they know they don't have quite as long on earth to be acting a fool, so they want to taint everyone they come in contact with their miserable life, and misery loves company. Anyone that has time to sit and talk on the telephone all day about every-body's business but their own, they are miserable and don't have a life. Most ladies never take the time to look at how they contributed to their life not being the way that they wanted it to be. They had a part in it but they don't want to own up to it; they just want to be

41

able to play the blame game because it has been working for them. They're stuck in the same spot and can't figure out why. It has been everyone's fault but theirs and most of these women have the nerve to call someone else stupid or crazy.

Why is it so hard for women just to be themselves and stop pretending? Will some women never grow up? We know that all women are not like this:

- They are the women that have not taken the time and effort to accomplish and meet their own goals.

- They are the women who have spent a lifetime living his dream on his promises when he didn't even want them, and they even knew it.

- They are the women that hold envy, jealously, and strife in their hearts because they settled for less.

- They are the women that thought they were fooling every-one, but only made a fool of themselves.

- They are the women who sit back and talk about everyone else.

- They are the women that can see everyone's wrong doing except their own.

- They are the women who have broken up marriages and now wonder why their own marriage is not working or if they'll ever be married.

- They are the women that have had countless men and still feel empty inside.

- They are the women who have played games all their life and now the tables have turned.

- They are the women that smile in your face but talk about you behind your back.

- They are the women who never wanted to work for any-thing in life, and now they think everyone else thinks that they are better than them.

- They are the women who have spent over half their lives in the clubs and still go home alone or with a different man every time.

- They are the women who have had a house full of kids, thinking that this was going to keep him but he still left.

These are just a few examples of women who don't know how to stand up and be themselves; they always have to hide behind something or someone. Once you decide to rise up and be yourself, you don't have to be phony because the only thing that is going to stand is whatever is right. It is always a good idea to start with yourself. It is called self examination, everyone needs to examine themselves first before you can move on. Take the time to stop and think about the choices in your life that you are making before you actually make them. Be aware and ready to deal with the consequences. Stop blaming others for your mishaps because no one can make us do anything, we do it because we want to. If you don't like the way you look and you can change it, then do so and move on. Life is short, why would anyone want to spend a whole lifetime pretending to be someone they are not? There is only one you, which means you are the original copy, why be fake and phony? What are you afraid of? Who put fear in your heart to make you feel that you are not good enough to be yourself? Loose the low self esteem, rise up, be yourself, and strive for the best. Beauty is only skin deep, be nice and kind to people; it goes a long way. Treat others the way you would like to be treated because however you treat people you will surely get it back in return, and stay away from cliques of so-called friends. If you don't have true friends, ask yourself what they want from you. Just look around and see how many of your so-called friends are still in your corner from many, many years ago. Okay! You have your final answer, they come and they go, so what does that tell you?

Have you ever noticed that most of the people in the cliques never get anywhere in life? This tells us a whole lot because if just one of them decided to use their own mind and think, they would no longer be excepted in the clique. Take the time to think about all the people who betrayed you; at some point in time in your life you really thought they were your friend. They are now no longer around! What happened? You know what happened; they were phony. Stop going through life looking for friends because if GOD places someone in your life this will be the only way it will work. People only come into your life for a reason, a season, or a lifetime; you have to admit most of the people that you have met are no longer in your life because it was only for a reason and a season. Don't be upset, they were never meant to stay because if they were it would have been for a lifetime.

So-called friends are just people that want to know everything that goes on in your life; they are not going to contribute to anything, they just want to be nosy, because they don't have anything else to do. True friends don't betray each other. Why waste a lifetime thinking you got friends and trusting everyone with your situations but GOD. GOD is the only one that never tells your business and until you come to that conclusion you will forever be mislead and betrayed by people, especially people you thought were your so-called friends. Most women can't stand each other, so how on earth are they going to be friends with you and be on your side? Open your eyes women, the devil comes in many disguises, but unfortunately he plays the same games!

This is the reason many women feel that they have to be phony: so they can be accepted—but wake up; it is a trick of the devil. If you can't be yourself, what are you good for? The true you will surface; it is just a matter of time. Stop listening to everything you hear people say, and just watch the things that they do; their ways and actions will tell you everything you need to know about them. Just pay attention, it never fails. It is what it is; if it looks like a snake, believe it. Whatever is deep down in their hearts will come out of their mouth at some point and then you will know that GOD has given you the warnings and the signs of who this person really is. At this time you will either continue to hang with them and get bit by them, or just pray for them and move on; the things that they do override everything that they say. These are things that keep women in the same position for many years of their life and they don't realize why they can't ever get what they have asked GOD for.

For everything that happens in our life there is a reason, and a lesson behind it. At what point in our life do we actually take heed and ask GOD to help us change our ways and heart? This is out of our control and everyone really knows it deep down inside. Stop looking for people to do what is right when you know what is deep in their hearts because they have already shown you. Just knowing that we were made from dirt should tell everyone a whole lot if they really paid attention to things. It is not in some of our hearts to even think about doing what is right just because it is right. On the other hand, many people are phony because they are not even aware of who they really are. Many people hide behind drugs, alcohols, food, etc., afraid to be themselves for whatever reason. It appears the some are even afraid of themselves. What causes this? Lack of knowledge, not realizing that without GOD nobody knows their own name, which means we can't do anything without GOD. Many people think that they are actually doing things on their own and accomplishing goals on their own, like they really have sense enough to do that. They never stop to think who really woke them up this morning, or does that even matter as long as they get what they want, whenever they want it? How are we so easy to forget about GOD until we get in trouble; GOD is just like we are, "don't just use me (GOD) when you want something!" GOD feels the same way, yes he is a jealous GOD, so why keep putting things, people, etc., before him? Have you ever noticed what happens when you do this? If you have noticed what happens when you do this, then why are you still doing it, but looking for different results? The results will be the same every time you do this. If you are tired of being phony, try GOD; he will teach you how to be yourself and love yourself.

I think it is true to say that everyone has the opportunity to make their own beds, they just don't realize that at some point in their life they will have to lie in it. This is the part of life that no one wants to live up too because at the time they were making their bed no one was thinking and considering the consequences that come with the choices that they were making. Don't get me wrong; we all know sometimes life can seem unfair, but GOD is fair. This is the reason we have to be very careful how we treat people because what goes around does comes back around. Be careful how you entertain a stranger. If possible try to be nice to people because we don't know who might have to come to our rescue one day. You would think this would make everyone a little bit more concerned of others considering that we all are walking on this journey and no one knows what lies ahead in his or her life. Furthermore, we don't know who's help we might need, and most of the time it will be the person that you least expect, and the ones you mistreated the most, so be careful! The journey of life is not easy and it was never meant to be, when everyone starts out there will be detours, turns, setbacks, etc., but the key is to stay in the race. As long as we can remember and keep in mind that we have the opportunity to chose right or wrong choices in our own life, it is wise to chose carefully because there are consequences, whether good or bad, that come along with the choices you make. When we make unwise choices be prepared to deal with the consequences and don't blame it on the world. Always remember GOD is with us all the way, it is impossible to travel on this journey without GOD because you will surely need him in order to make it through. You can pretend that you are doing things on your own all you want to, all you have to do is just keep on living. GOD will show you exactly how far you can make it without him. Which is nowhere, you are continually making circles around yourself and you are so dizzy and you don't even know it. Ladies, wake up! Open your eyes, it is spelled out right before our eyes. It is what it looks like. Don't try to change it, you will find yourself sliding in hell on first base trying to change something that was never meant to be.

"PRAY FOR DELIVERANCE AND GOD WILL DELIVER YOU!"

Chapter 8

Facing Life The Way It Is

Accepting life the way it is can be hard at times for people, especially those that don't believe in GOD. When we believe in GOD and realize that he is in control of everything and everybody, you don't really worry about the things that are out of your control, because you are aware that you can't handle or change them anyway. There are many of us that really don't know GOD, we know of GOD, but there is a big difference. This is what confuses many but very few try to get to know the difference. We all go through trials and tribulations throughout our entire life and we need to remember that no one is eliminated, but they are only to make us stronger, not to kill us. If we are honest with ourselves we have to admit that it does make us a better person every time. It teaches us what to do and what not to do, and who to deal with and who not to deal with. This is how we are taught on our journey throughout life about life as well as people. Sometimes, I do agree, it doesn't feel good and times get to be really tough. But through it all, someway somehow we still make it through—and why is that? That's because GOD had already promised us that he would always be with us and never leave us. So through it all GOD keeps us in our right mind to deal with the situation until the next one comes along. Not if, but *when* the next trial comes along—but this is all part of the journey that we are on day-by-day, trying our best to make it. Real life. A huge percentage of women have been abused and misused all across the world. Whether it was physical or mental, abuse is abuse. There is no way to dress it up; this is what many women go through because they are living in denial. This is what makes it hard for many to face life the way it is.

Ruby J. Davis

Being a victim of abuse causes you to lose confidence and self esteem, although by the grace of GOD, once you are out of it you can gain it back. This is something that doesn't take place over-night; it is a process of gaining a part of you back that someone took from you who was never worthy of you anyway. It can be hard to face life the way it is sometimes until you actually heal. The healing process requires time and patience plus getting to know yourself and getting to know GOD better. For the ladies that don't get out of it (the ones quickest to say he never gave me a black eye), they don't realize they have a black heart—which is terrible, because now everyone they meet will have to pay for something someone else is doing to them. If you look at the overall picture, you can see that there is not much difference in abuse because all of it makes you feel the same way—hurt from within your heart and empty inside. It might stem from different actions, but the end results are the same: a broken heart and a messed up mind. So who really is fooling who?

I can speak about this because I have been a victim of domestic violence and lived through it and have been healed and delivered from it. And no it was not easy, but with GOD all things are pos-sible. For the women in the world that have never had to endure anything like it, please know that it is truly a blessing from GOD, because the numbers are few. The more and more experiences in life that we go through should teach us to chose wisely. Life is full of challenges, I agree, but there are some things that we bring on our-selves, especially if we have already been through it and know the outcome. Some of us don't learn as fast as others; we always feel that this person will be so much different until we realize we see the very same traits—he just has a different face, a different name and a different address. After being tainted for so many years, it can make it hard to face reality because you have lived in denial so long it seems normal to you.

But what is normal? Many women get to the point where they actually feel that they don't have a choice, and this is when they can't face life the way it is because they don't really know how. Being abused does not let you think for yourself, it allows the per-son or people abusing you to think and dictate for you. Once you get used to it, then it becomes the norm for you, until you learn better.

It is truly amazing how many men are abusive to women, have either been around it all their lives or was in the home where it was taking place. However it happened, it rubbed off on them and they feel that it is the right thing to do. Society looks at it and reasons with it at times because they can say that this is all the individual knows, because this is what they became accustomed to. But whatever happened to the men who were around real men that got up and worked every day, treated their wives like real woman, even in their home on a daily basis—and now they don't want to work. Why didn't that rub off? So at what point can we determine that people become whatever environment they are accustom to? Could it be just something that they chose to do just to control that person? It is really hard to determine why a person is abusive and I am aware that some women are abusive as well, but only that person can answer to why they like to fight and hurt other people. We can't determine that because of what environment they were brought up in or were around because that is not always the case. If we look at things that happen in the world today we can see for ourselves that some of the people that grew up in the worst environment have succeeded in life, versus someone growing up who had it all, and never had to want for anything and now they don't have anything and don't want anything.

There has to be a deeper reason why people do what they do, and only that individual can answer that. Everybody thinks differently and acts differently, and so it is hard to tell what makes a person do what they do. Abuse doesn't have an age on it, some old people are still being abusive after twenty, thirty years of marriage or more, but only the abuser can answer why have they been abusing their spouses for all those years (and yet they'll swear up and down that they truly love them).

Is it possible that abuse is just like a drug, it is something that they feel that they just have to do? Drug addicts and alcoholics are labeled as being sick, can we say the same thing about a person that is abusive? This is a million dollar question because no one wants to wear the label that they are sick and need help but what is the difference—if you are sick you are sick; it doesn't matter what your sickness might be. No one can get help in those situations unless the they them self want it and realize that they do need help. No one can make the individual get help, this has to come from the individual's heart, and until they get the help that they need they will not be delivered from the evil things that they are doing to hurt other people. There is nothing that just goes away, everything that goes away there is some sort of process involved with it. Until they realized that they can't do it on their own, they will never stop doing what they are doing because they are trying to do it by themselves. If we are nothing without GOD, how can we do it by ourselves? We can't and this is the reason innocent people are continually getting abused and misused. We all have to wake up and face the truth; we can't do anything on our own, without GOD's help. There is a reason he promised us that he would never leave us alone; GOD knows we can't handle these situations on our own. Many have tried over, and over again but the end result remains the same—so that has to tell us something. Why does that seem really hard to grasp, how many times do we have to keep going through the same thing looking for better or different results? It will never happen. Many people are never the same after abuse: they have been messed up for life. But who can we blame? Who do we point the finger at without fingers being pointed back at us; many say people can only do what you allow them to do, so who do we blame! That is a tough question that many will chose not to answer because no one can give a feasible answer to it. One thing about life is, the abuser does have to deal and live with conse-quences down the line for what they have done. No one gets away with the bad choices that they make, many have even had their lives taken in return. Why would anyone in their right mind think that they can always just do whatever and treat people however they want and think that nothing will ever happens to them? Could this be a sickness as well? Nothing in life remains the same; GOD is the only one that doesn't change. GOD is the same yesterday, today and forever more. Everything and everybody else will change. It's not if, but when.

Life is nothing but full-time school, which means some gradu-ate and some don't but everyone has an opportunity to learn if they choose to. Many are looking for shortcuts, but we have all lived long enough to know the short cuts don't work. This is something that we see on a daily basis. However there are so many still try-ing, thinking that they can actually master the shortcuts. Everyone will graduate at different times, it doesn't matter if they started out at the same time or not. You have to endure to the very end to get your cap and gown. It is not suppose to be easy, because nothing in life that is worth having is going to be easy. Just as sure as you live long enough, everyone will have a sad story to tell—but that is okay, because if you have the sad story, that means that you lived through it and can move on. Always remember: no story no glory! From day to day on this journey no one knows what will happen tomorrow. Life is full of swift transitions at any given time; we just have to be prepared to make the transitions when we least expect them. Of course we don't know what they might be, because GOD already knows. If we knew how we would respond—this is the rea-son it is such a mystery. And even if we did know what could we actually do about something that was going to happen anyway?

GOD saves us the trouble of worrying ahead of time, because he knew it would be too overwhelming to deal with all at once. This is the reason we should only take one day at a time, and enjoy that day and not worry about tomorrow because it is not promised to anyone and most of us can't handle our tomorrow on today any-way. Tomorrow always has a new set of problems and situations. If we take the time and slow our lives down we will be able to make the connections in life that GOD wants us to make. We will be able to see why some things didn't happen when we thought it should of happened, because everything will go according to GOD's plans; it doesn't matter what U-turns and detours you decide to take, the final plan will be GOD's plan. Have you ever noticed how there were some things that you tried your best to make work and it never worked? What does that tell you? You prayed over and over for the same thing and then you finally got it. That's because it will only fall within GOD's plan for your life. Other than that we are just making a mess of everything and can't figure out why it is not going the way we want or think it should go. It is not our plan, it is GOD's plan, when we realize this we can face any obstacles that comes our way and realize that it is in GOD's hand—which means everything will be okay, don't worry. Just Relax!

"RISE UP ~ BE YOURSELF!"

Chapter 9

Life Is What You Make Out of It

What a true statement. Life is exactly what you make out of it. If you don't want anything you will get absolutely nothing in return, because no one is going to *give* you anything! You have to earn it, and most of the time it will be the hard way. This is why we have to set our own goals and try our best to accomplish them because no one else really cares. Everyone has goals of their own and are focusing on them; we have to be realistic and stop looking to get something for nothing because it doesn't happen that way. We don't have to give up on our dreams and goals just because they sometimes seems unreachable or really hard to meet, but as long as we keep striving for bigger and better we will eventually accomplish them.

Unfortunately most of the time you will be on your own and will not get a lot of encouragement. We have to learn how to encourage ourselves and keep on moving because in the meantime we are still walking our challenging journey, and the trials and tribulations will still be arising in our life as we go. This makes the process more difficult, but it is still achievable if you are willing to take the challenges. Don't let anyone or anything allow you to give up on you or your goals, because anything that is worth having is going to be a challenge to achieve. If you are hanging around people and they don't want anything out of life, your best bet is to leave them alone and move on. People can actually hold back your progress in life if you allow them too. Everybody has different goals and dreams so don't let anyone detour you from yours just because it seems unrealistic to them. When we allow people to enter into our lives most of the time they already have a set agenda and sometimes it can get you totally off track without thinking. We have to be careful not to let people waste our time we have to ask ourselves — are they worth it? We all are different, and think differently, so don't expect everyone to be proud of your accomplishments when they have not even tried to meet their own. It is not going to happen; people are not really happy for you when you accomplish some of your goals because they know they have had the same or even better opportunities, yet did nothing with them.

After you start accomplishing some of your goals, you really can't hang around with some of the same people that you use to hang with. They no longer are going to view you the same and they will flip the script on you and tell you that you are acting differently now, when all the time it is not you but them; don't let them fool you! You came to a conclusion and realized that your so-called friends didn't want anything out of life but what they were getting, so you decided to change your surroundings to positive things, and positive people similar to yourself. What sense does it make to be mad at someone because they want something better out of life and you don't? It happens all the time, everywhere we go, old and young people have this same negative attitude. It is called people being people and having something negative to say about everything. Have you noticed that most of the people that do all the talking hardly ever get anything completed? If you are going to do something, just do it — you don't need anyone else's opinion about it; they can't and will not help you anyway. We spend a whole lot of time and energy trying to hear someone else's opinion about different matters in our life, but they don't care what we do, especially when there is nothing in it for them. Save your breath and just do it. Follow your own mind and heart; people don't really mean us any good anyway, it's all about what they can get out of us and if that is nothing they quickly throw you to the side and move on to the next one.

Stop settling for less just because you think that you may lose a so-called friend; you don't really have true friends anyway, it just appears that away for now. The longer you keep walking on your journey you will find out for yourself, and this happens to be the best way, since you would not listen to anyone else who tried to tell you. Life can be as simple as we allow it to be, or it can be as complicated as we want it to be. We can listen and take advice from people who have already been there and done that and already have an idea of the end result, or we can try it on our own and hope and look for different results. The choice is all yours, everyone has the pleasure of making their own bed, because they will surely have the pleasure to lie in it as well. Life is all about choices, which is something we all play a part in. We just have to be ready for what comes along, and not blame other people.

If there is anyone in your life that you know who has become successful, you should take the time to hear their story, because it was quite a challenge getting to the position where they are. There is always a sad story behind anyone's GLORY! Because as we know, nobody gave them anything; they earned it. For the ones that really didn't earn it there is a possibility they may not be able to maintain it. You can accomplish almost anything that you might want out of life; just be prepared for the processes that you will have to go through, and never give up on your dreams and goals. Stop living in other people dreams and have your own; everyone has that opportunity. The key is to be willing to make the sacrifices. If you can see it, more than likely you can achieve it, because no one can stop you but you. So if you have lived and now you are old and you feel that you didn't accomplish your dreams, go to the mirror and take a real good look at who you see staring back at you. It was you that stopped you – don't try to blame it on anyone else. You did it all by yourself; now you can get over it and move on and be happy for someone younger that you see trying to fulfill their dream. Life goes on with or without you and we only get one shot it; one shot at being young, and if we live we get a shot at being old. Stop trying to fool yourself that you can do the same thing as you did when you were young when you have gotten older, because it is not so. First of all you have to be realistic with yourself, and then you can accept everything else as it comes. There are many older people that have actually blown every chance or opportunity, and now they realize that they can't get that time back. And they also feel that they don't have much longer to live, so they are disappointed at the whole world. They are disappointed because they played around when others were actually working toward their goals, and they thought someone was going to give them something on a silver platter. What a waste to go through your entire life to find out you didn't fool anyone but yourself! It happens, and we see these type of people everywhere we go, and we hear people always talking about, "what they should have done." So ask yourself, who ever stopped you in the first place?

You get back the same thing that you give out. So if you are wondering why you never got anything — what have you ever done to help someone else along this journey? Whatever you give away it does comes back to you. GOD don't bless us for ourselves, GOD blesses us to be a blessing to someone else. This is the reason we are all here together, because we need each other to survive. At some point in life everyone is going to need someone and we never know who it might be, so it really pays to be nice to people, because it is the right thing to do. If you spend your life playing games and taking short cuts, you will not get anything in return. Ask your so-called friends that have played games all their lives. We all can find a reason or excuse for everything that has happened in our life, but who cares about that? On November 4, 2008, this was a good enough reason for anybody to realize that excuses are not acceptable anymore. Why are there so many people afraid, and afraid of what? There is nothing to it but to do it, how bad do you want it? Life is beautiful and we only live once, so why do you choose to stop yourself from obtaining your own dreams and happiness? This is your responsibility, not anyone else's. If you are waiting on someone else to make you happy, you have the wrong idea. You will die first; everyone is looking out for and focusing on themselves. All we have to do is stand up and be counted. Stand for what is right because it is right, and everything else will follow. Stop being afraid of failure, nothing fails but a try. So what if you fail the first time or even the second time, it doesn't matter. What matters is you were willing to try and if you keep on trying you will be successful but you can't give up just because it is not coming easy. Nothing in life is easy, if it came easy, more than likely you will have to suffer the consequences the rest of your life for it.

Success does not come easy at all, nor does it come over night, just ask someone who is successful! You know when you are on the right track when all of your so-called friends have betrayed you along the way. This is the motivation and strength that is needed to make us want to keep going and striving. Most of the people that actually have became successful had to do almost everything by themselves, because others didn't believe in them and were really afraid and jealous of them, because they knew that they would make it someday, they just didn't know when it would take place.

On the other hand, they also knew they were not going to help and inspire them in no kind of way, hoping that they would give up because they were the ones that were afraid to take the challenges. This seems to be what so-called friends are really good for: discouragements and disappointments.

It is time for you to set yourself apart and live your life; get off the phone and go to the throne. There is always a price that you will have to pay if you have dreams and goals that you would like to accomplish, because no one is going to view things the way that you do; to them you must be crazy. People are quick to call other people crazy, but it is not being crazy; it is being different. Thinking differently, seeing things differently and wanting something different from what they are use to getting in life. If you want to label this as being crazy, it is okay, because the world is full of crazy successful people. Just turn your TV on! Have you even wondered why you are watching them on TV and they are not watching you, now who really is crazy?

"MAKE YOUR CHOICES WISELY AND SOBER MINDED, BECAUSE YOU HAVE TO LIVE WITH THE CONSEQUENCES!"

Chapter 10

How to Get Beyond Our Past

The Bible tells us that everyone has sinned and fallen short of the glory of GOD. Many of us have been hurt and disappointed by someone who was close to us. We still have to learn to forgive and forget and move on with our life; no one said this would be easy, but until we do it we will forever live in our past. We also have to examine our own lives. How many people have we actually hurt? When it comes back around we get the opportunity to see how it really felt. It will not kill us, it will only make us stronger and allow us to think twice before we do things to people that we don't want done to us. By now many of us realize that we are on a journey, traveling through life trying to make it to the end. Most of us have also concluded that there are only two paths to follow; we will either follow the right path or the wrong path. Unfortunately, there is no in-between, some just think there is. But we get to choose. It doesn't get any better than that; we actually have a choice of which way we want to go. There might be many that can't see it so clearly right now, but just keep on traveling; someday it will come to you why nothing is going right in your life and then you will be able to figure it out. We all make mistakes and we all are human, but once we realize that we are going the wrong direction it is time to turn around. Everyone knows that no one is perfect, but how many times are we going to keep using this excuse, and keep going the same route, and keep getting bitten by the same type of snakes— still looking for different results?

We all are struggling with something every day of our lives and it doesn't matter what it might be, but it is real life events we have to get over it and move on. A lot of things that happen in our life we don't have a say-so about; we just have to live with it. Stop analyzing and rationalizing with yourself and asking, why me? Because the question can easily be reversed, why not you? What have you done so great here on earth to be eliminated from trials and tribulations? It might not be your turn right now, but just keep on walking—everyone gets a turn at it. This is what makes us stronger and wiser and also helps us to continue our journey and realize that we need GOD to travel this journey, because we can't do it by ourselves. Although some might think that they can, but it is always a matter of time before GOD reveals Himself and lets them know—we are nothing without Him. Once we can get past all the bad things that have taken place in our lives, we will be able to live and look forward to the future. We have to focus on the good, because the good outweighs the bad in most cases. We have to learn to leave the past in the past. I know sometimes it can be hard to forget, but until we decide to move on and forgive we will forever dwell in our past and ruin it for our future.

Again the choice is totally up to us, we have a choice in whatever we decide to make of our own lives. Don't be disappointed at other people just because you are bitter, holding grudges and hatred in your heart, and you can't let go of your past. Life is short; we only get one trip here on earth, so it is up to you, whatever you decide to do. If everyone is realistic with themselves they should realize that some day we are all going to die, so in knowing this why would you want to continue to live in the past?

Everyday that GOD wakes us up we get new grace and mercy; everyone one of us must get right whatever we know that we are doing wrong. Until we try to do the right thing because it is right, our future will seem as though there isn't one. Forgetting our past may consist of leaving people behind or not dealing with certain people that we used to, but that's okay because they don't mean us any good anyway. If we are honest with ourselves, some of our so-called friends are the ones that have kept us in our past. Only GOD can change people, and he changes people everyday, but many people always have to bring up what we use to do in the past. If you know that you have changed your lifestyle stop hanging around those same people that you use to hang with. Leave them behind and keep on moving; we all know what GOD has done in our lives, so don't let anyone fool you—they are just mad because they have yet to be delivered. After we have lived to be a certain age, we have to realize that nothing is new; the game is old, it is just different faces with different names, but the games remain the same. The Bible tells us that nothing is new under the sun, so why are we so surprised when certain things come our way in life? There is nothing new, but it might be new to you—but someone has already had to deal with it and conquered it and moved on and so can you. When it comes to real life trials and tribulations there is no discrimination—everyone gets a shot at the good, the bad, and the ugly. If you haven't yet, just keeping waking up every morning. All we have to do is keep on living. It might be your next door neighbor now, but as life goes on it could easily be you. We can't get comfortable because no one knows what the next day may hold but the almighty GOD, and if you don't know Him this means you are lost in the wilderness and don't know which way to go.

For many of us forgetting our past means to keep walking and don't look back regardless of what has taken place. As long as we are looking back we can't see clearly ahead. We have to move beyond the disappointments and live our life to the fullest. We spend enough time not knowing or realizing how good GOD is, but when we finally find out we should act upon it and live our life as best we can. Try not to worry about how people did you wrong or mistreated you, because more than likely somewhere on your journey you did someone wrong as well. Stop fooling yourself that you have forgiven people when you know you haven't; until you forgive them you will not be able to move forward. There is nothing about life that's going to be easy, so why do we expect for it to be and get disappointed and discouraged when it is not? No one actually told you that life was going be easy; this was just something that you assumed because you never really knew what other people went through to get to where they are now. Yes, it was a struggle and it will be a struggle because anything worth having is going to cost you sometimes more than you might be willing to pay at times, but it will be well worth it in the end. When we are trying to get beyond our past, in most cases we will be left alone. But this is a good sign, because this means that you are leaving the excess baggage behind and can now make progress because your load is much lighter. If you find yourself really standing alone, please don't get discouraged; that just means it is time to let your light shine. Now you can focus better on your future and strive to reach your goals without constantly going back into your past. It is truly amazing how life can be as simple as we want it to be, and we spend most of our life making things so complicated when the bottom line is usually ourselves — what choices we make and how we deal with the consequences. In many situations there is no one to blame but ourselves, no one can hurt us as bad as we can hurt our own selves, so what is the real problem? The real problem is most of us are focusing on the wrong things and missing the entire point of life in general. We are so worried and afraid that the next person is going to do so much better than we are that we end us losing focus on what is really important and what we suppose to be doing. We are so afraid that we might accidently help someone accomplish their goals when we haven't accomplished our own.

We spend a lot of time trying to figure out and take care of everyone else's business but our own. And when we look around we have already lived to be half a hundred, gray hair is starting to set in, and nothing is working for us yet, and we wonder why! Take care of your own business and stop trying to figure out other people's, because there are not enough hours in the day to do both. This is just another way we allow things to hold us back. GOD is not going to get anyone's blessing mixed up; whatever is for you, it is for you, and no devil in hell can take it away. Relax! Mind your own issues and leave other people's business alone. Stop wasting your time trying to get even with the devil; it is endless — get off the phone and go to the throne. When we go through life and continue to go through trials and tribulations while on our journey, we do get to the point and realization that we can't live on anyone's promises but GOD's. This is always the bottom line, so leave everything in the past and keep going and striving toward the great future that GOD has promised you. This is how we get beyond the obstacles in our past and are able to move forward with our lives. We just have to make up our minds and do it even though sometimes it can feel like it is not the right time. If you have thought about it, it is the right time: "<u>ain't nothing to it but to do it</u>." The key is to stay focused on whatever your goals may be, because everyone has some type of goal, large or small. Focus on it and move toward as much as you can and you will eventually accomplish it. The more you stay focused on your goals the more you will be able to leave your past in the past. Don't get caught up in people and let them tell you what you can and cannot do. "We all can do all through Christ who strengthens us." Don't let people fool you because they don't know; always keep in mind that people do perish because of lack of knowledge, and age didn't have anything to do with it. All we have to do is look around us or turn on the TV. It is what it is!

"Leave The Past In The Past And Walk Into Your Future!"

Chapter 11

The Type of People to Stay Away From

On our journey through life we get to meet all types of people; some are good and some not so good. We have to learn to tolerate all types of people because everyone is different and acts differently. Everyone believes they are normal and nothing is wrong with them; it is always the next person. Everyone was raised by different people, so we all act differently and have different moral values. So we should not be discouraged when we see people who really don't have our same values, because they were never taught some things. Many times it is not their fault that they were not taught, but they just happen to be the lost victim. We know sometimes we get fooled by a first impression, but we must remember when GOD reveals to us how they really are, to believe GOD, pray for them, and leave them alone. Please take heed that we can't change them; this job is much too hard for us. That is the reason it is GOD's job, because he knows it is impossible for us to change someone. Although many have and will die in the trying too, because they just don't get it.

This is a big mistake we make in life, a mistake that can have an effect on our entire life, not paying attention to what GOD is allowing us to see about who and how people really are. GOD always has a way of letting us know how the people are that we meet and are dealing with, good or bad. Sometimes we miss the first sign that he gives us, but just keep on looking; he will show you another and another until you get it. Once you finally see, please leave them alone, pray for them and keep on going. There are reasons why some people cross our path but we can't say it is GOD all the time because the devil has his workers on the battlefield as well, placing people cross our path. I truly believe if it is GOD that had that person to cross our path we will learn something positive to help us on our journey. If it is the devil everything is negative; we want to forget we ever met that person and pray we never see them again. This is really when we have to be careful because everyone is in disguise for some reason and you really don't know how and who they are until they actually show you. When they show you, it is what it is believe them, pray for them and keep on going. We can't judge them by how they look or what they say, because this will mislead us every single time. Ways and actions tells us everything we need to know about people and some of them have not figured that out yet. Why not? Because they are lost and they really think and believe in their own hearts that they are fooling people, when all the time they are only fooling themselves. It is real life, what can we say? Some will get it and some will not. We have to know what type of people to stay away from by what our expectations are and what we want in the future for our own lives. We don't need any side trackers because we will meet many of them on this journey and they might not even be aware that they are side trackers for us—although many of them do know because they know what their agenda is from the very beginning. But we will know because GOD will reveal the side trackers that don't want anything and don't want you to have anything.

For instance, if you are waiting for a spouse, please don't waste your time around older women who hate their spouses of twenty, thirty, forty years etc. and they are always all by themselves and never with him. To think they have the nerve to wonder why their own husbands don't want to be around them, and all they do is put him down. These type of people are not very good role models; leave them in the past where they are living. Don't waste your time with people who are jealous of you; keep going, because they are a snake and if you continue to hang around them you will get bit. When a person cannot look you in the eye while holding a conversation with you, run! They are hiding something very important. When people pretend they are perfect and have done no wrong at all, run! They are sickly and don't even know it. When you are around people that go to church and say they read their Bible all day long and pray all day long every day, run! More than likely they can't comprehending what they are reading, they are leaning to their own understanding and they do not believe that GOD hears them when they pray. They are totally confused and if you stick around them long enough you will be too. Stay away from people that think just because they never used drugs or drank alcohol they have not sinned and did no wrong, run from them! Because their issues are much deeper than drugs and alcohol and you really don't want to know what they really do or did. If your so-called friends can never compliment you or congratulate you, leave them alone; they are not your friends; they envy you. Try your best to stay away from negative people because most of them are in denial and are lost, and guess what—age doesn't have anything to do with it. If people are sixty-five and older and still think that they are young, leave them alone; something is wrong with them and it is not your job to figure it out. If you meet people and they think you are crazy and they are getting over on you, leave them alone because they have been doing this their entire lives and more than likely don't have a life, because they are lost and think no one can see through them. Stay away from seasoned people that have lived over half of their life, say they have been serving and walking with GOD for decades, and still don't know their purpose is here on earth. One can't help but to wonder why GOD hasn't revealed it to them yet, or are there really serving just GOD!

Ladies, if you meet a man and all he talks about is how much of a real man he is, run! Because he is in denial and probably never has had a real women. Real men don't have to express themselves like that. For the most part, real men keep their mouth closed, they pay attention and they know what to say, how to say it, and when. Real men recognize a prize when they see it and will not disrespect it in no kind of way, and if they happen to ask for your telephone number, they will gladly use it and not try to run games. They will treat you the way they would like to be treated. If you meet a man and he can't even tell you where he lives and all he can give you is his cell phone number leave him alone; he is running a game but he is only playing himself. If you have so-called friends that want to call you all the time with their problems but never have time to listen to yours, leave them alone; you can't help them and they can't help you—so stop wasting all your precious time on the telephone. Get off of the phone and go to the throne! If your so-called friend always want to hang around you and your spouse and she is not married, leave her alone because as soon as you turn your back she will be in your front door, pretending that she is looking for you. Stay away from people that are always making promises and not keeping any, but always are talking about what they're "GONNA" do, but never make any effort to actually do anything. Stay away from people that always say I will get you something later, the intent is never to get you anything; your birthday comes on the same date every year and they know this, so what is the real problem? If you call or e-mail your so-called friend for days and they never get back to you until weeks and weeks later, leave them alone, no one is that busy and everyone has a caller ID, they don't want to be bothered but what they don't realized is, "neither do you." You were just trying to be nice. If you only hear from people once in a blue moon, what do they want? They only want to be nosy because you could have been dead for all they know. When you run into so-called saints and they never wear a smile, just tilt your hat or give them a salute and keep on going, don't get mad because it is not about yo—they are mad at themselves. Pray for them and keeping on moving. When you come in contact with people and they have different attitudes all the time, don't waste your time trying to figure them out, GOD has yet to deliver them; just pray for them and keep going. Don't waste your time with people that don't believing in helping the less fortunate ones, because GOD already told us the poor will be with us always. Stay away from people that don't believing in giving and helping other people. If you are not sure about some of the people that you meet, just ask GOD; he will show you what you need to see exactly when you need to see it; so don't worry if you don't know yet—just keep on looking and living. Life gets better and better, especially when you are able to see people for who they really are. And they not even aware of it, because they think they are fooling someone—when all the time they are only making a fool out of themselves.

Life is really beautiful, but you have to treat people right in order to reap the benefits and have peace of mind. We have to come in contact with all different types of people so we can see just how blessed we are to actually be in our right mind. Everyone is not in their right mind, so we have to be thankful; GOD allows us the opportunity to see something of everything in life, and all kinds of people so we can appreciate life as it is and who we are as a person. We are given opportunities to come in contact with different people to help us grow, because unfortunately there will be many people that will never get it and really understand life, but they are still blessed as well and JESUS loves them also. GOD blesses every single one of us, so there is really no reason to complain about anything. GOD knows what he is doing, we just have to trust and believe him that everything will be okay. He is in control of everything and everybody, although some people just might not be aware of it yet. So why do we get so stressed when things don't go our way or when people do us wrong? Because some of us are not there yet. GOD sees everything so there is no need to worry, he has everything under control regardless of how your situation looks. No one gets away with anything, for GOD will bring every deed into judgment, including every hidden thing, whether it is good or evil, so don't worry about anything. GOD has everything on record. Trust me when I say, GOD got this!

Please, whatever you do, stay away from people that are always in hurry. Why? Because without directions where are they going? They are not going anywhere, just making circles around themselves. If they are too busy for you, you already know they don't have time for GOD, so let them go on down the road because they can't help you anyway. Everyone is so busy and always running for what? If you are that busy it is impossible for you to have time for GOD or even yourself. Could this be because they are running from themselves? What do people in a hurry really accomplish? Not much of anything because they are too busy to ever get the results.

Although these are many examples of people to stay away from, we have to learn from them as well. I have to assume that they also learn something from us. We just have to learn to stay in our lane, and not get caught up with the wrong set of people. We have to remember that everyone has an agenda, and no one really knows what that agenda is but the individual themselves. Life teaches us to be very careful what we say, who we say it to and who we deal with, because everyone is someone's "undercover detective and representative," believe it or not. The key is just to try to keep a clean slate; you can't go wrong because people will always be people no matter what. Everyone knows by now that you can't please people, and if they don't know, they just have to keep on living and one day they will find out as well. It has been said that people do whatever they want to do, so why not practice being nice to other people, and treat them the way that you would like to be treated, and see what happens? We all know that everybody is tired, because everyone that is living is working on something every day, the only people that really get the proper rest are the ones that are already dead and resting in their graves or on the shelf right now. So we can't keep using the excuse that we are tired; everyone is tired. Your job is whatever you do on a daily basis and yes, everyone has a different job to do, the only difference is that some of us get paid more than others—but we all get paid something. It just might not be money all the time for everyone. There is a reward in whatever we do, good or bad, but we get to choose and we get paid. We also need to realize that we can take something from every single person we come in contact with, whether good or bad, and use it for our own benefit. We all can find some good in some of the worst people that we have met, so we have to realize that nothing is in vain; we can use it to better ourselves.

Everyone is considered a teacher, meaning we all can learn something from everyone, whether it is good or bad, if we take the time to listen and stop running in a hurry not really going anywhere. It doesn't matter what type of people we meet, we have to remember it is not about us anyway. We are living in the wilderness and nothing is easy for anyone; this should teach us to help and appreciate one another. During our walk throughout the wilderness, times are going to get tough—but trouble doesn't last forever. Everyone will have their times and shares of trials and tribulations, no one is exempt. We just have to wait our turn. Trials and tribulations never have and never will discriminate. In the wilderness we will meet all types of people, but all we have to keep in mind is that while in the wilderness we will have real life experiences — but we are only passing through, so we don't have to take it personally because we are not here to stay. Everyone has a purpose, many will know what their purpose is and many will not, so know that we have to realize that many people don't know where they are going and don't have any direction at all. Which means we can't help everyone, and everyone can't help us. Anyone that doesn't have instructions or directions are not going anywhere, they are just existing and wandering in the wilderness, without a clue to what is really going on. We might come in contact with many people like this but all we have to do is pray for them and keep going, especially if they don't want to listen or want your help. Many are lost in the wilderness and they don't even know it so we have to be careful how we treat people; everyone is dealing with some type of battle, and it pays to nice to people even if they are not nice to you. It will pay off in the end; just remember you get back whatever you put out; it all comes back.

"Let God Be The Head Of Your Life He Will Direct Your Pathway!"

Chapter 12

Don't Take It Personally; It's Not About You

We were all conceived and born into this world, we didn't have a choice in who our parents were going to be, our gender, race, or sex, etc. Because this really doesn't matter to GOD, in GOD's eyes all of us are the same. As we walk our journey we will get misused, abused, talked about, etc., but we have to keep in mind it is not about us. Most of these things are what happens to innocent people trying to mind their own business while walking their journey, trying to do what is right to the best of their ability. Whether you are nice or not you will get hurt; it's all a part of your valley experiences while on your journey walk. This is what makes and molds us into the men and women that we become. At some point in our life some of us come to the conclusion that we want to get back into church, because we are tired of what the world has to offer or has done to us. The world will chew us up and spit us back out without any remorse. We knew that years and years ago we went to church with our parents, but some of us did stray away from it when we got older, until we decide to come back with hopes that we can have a better life and get better guidance about what is actually going on in our lives. When we finally decide to make up in our minds and turn our life over to CHRIST we do just that.

However, many of us do view the church as a hospital, we all have problems or issues to deal with. This is why many of us go to church, because we realize that we can't do it on our own. Everyone that goes to church has situations and unresolved issues, but the challenge comes when we get injured in the hospital. Why is this a challenge? Because no one expects to go to the hospital and get injured, we expect to go to the hospital to get healed and delivered. But we have to remember it is not about us. This is the only thing that will keep us going; if not we will fall by the wayside and we will surely be left behind. We have to look at it like this. If the church is somewhat like a hospital and we know that everyone has their own type of sickness, what can we really expect from them but an injury of some sort? We have to remember that disease is contagious! Although we did get injured out in the world, to get injuries in the hospital can be a harder pill to swallow. We just have to be aware that it can and will happen to the best of us. Many of us will get injured right there in the church by those that portray themselves as being saved and filled with the holy ghost. So don't take it personally; we have to remember it is not about us. It is all part of the journey walk; don't get discouraged, just keep walking.

It is about JESUS. Nothing in life is going to be easy and most people that we meet on our journey are going to do a great job in not making it easy, for the simple fact that people will always be people. It doesn't matter if they are in the church or out of the church, they are still people—with different types of sickness and agendas. I know at times we might think that just because people go to church they will be different for some reason, but this is not always true. Please don't ever put in your mind that all the people that go to church are saved, real and right. Just know and always remember: the devil goes to church every Sunday and even has the nerve to smile in your face pat you on your back; he never misses a beat, he is just that good. He is always on time; he will be there when you get there and he will leave out the door right with you, so be careful! But you will know him when you see him; just watch out, because most of the time he is right next to you! Many that are at the church are just as lost as the ones that are still sitting in the clubs and wandering out in the world; they just aren't aware of it. We can't take it personally, because it is not about us anyway. "People will perish because of lack of knowledge."

We have to learn to stop letting people disappoint us by relying on them instead of GOD; this is the reason we are always disappointed. When dealing with people, it never really matters until the shoe is on the other foot, unfortunately church folks even feel the same way. This is the reason we have to trust in GOD, and many times leave people alone. This journey that we are traveling is not just a simple field trip, it is called real life, and you will have real life events whether you want them or not — many already have your name on them. We will be faced with major decisions, really not knowing what to do or which way to go. We can only ask GOD. We can't take these decisions and issues to people; they can't help us anyway; they don't even know what to do about their own issues. GOD is the only one that will give us the proper directions. There are many people walking around empty as a wagon inside, and most of them are married — sad but it is true. So what does that tell you! They still have a void in their lives, because no one can fill that void but GOD. Some have tried drugs, alcohol, sex, etc. and still are empty inside, because nothing is going to fill that void but GOD. When you know you have tried everything else and still feel empty inside, that's GOD. So what else can it be? Ladies, some of us have jumped from man to man all our lives and all we have are sad stories to tell behind it and nothing positive to show. So what is it that our heart is longing for and a man can't fulfill? It has to be GOD! I know this might seem foreign to most of the women, especially the ones that don't know GOD for themselves, but you have to ask yourself, why do you feel so empty inside when it appears you have everything that you could possibly want? Only you can answer that correctly, but deep down inside you know the real truth.

It is time for us to stop putting our souls on the line for these no good men because it will cause us to go straight to hell and there is no turning back. Is he really worth that? Real men want wives, not women just to go to bed with. Every time you take a chance going to bed with a man that you are not married too, it is a complete setback in your life, not to mention your soul is at risk. I should not even have to go there about you ladies sleeping with someone else's spouse, you already know this is a dead-end situation because you have cursed yourself and don't even realize it. All you have to do is ask some of your so-called friends or just turn and look in the mirror, because only you and GOD know your deepest secrets. And remember: don't do to someone what you don't want done to you! Every woman knows she don't want no one else sleeping with her man; this is always off limits. So leave someone else's spouse alone. It is that simple! Don't try to make it complicated because he isn't what you thought he was. Who's choice was it to marry him in the first place—or was he already married when you actually met him? Only you can answer that. The truth will set you free!

Don't get disappointed when things are not going the way you think they should. Take a look at how it all started at the very beginning of your relationship, and this will give you your final answers—to all the problems, sleepless nights, headaches, heartaches and complications that you have had to endure. We have to stand up for our mistakes and unwise choices and stop blaming other people. The bottom line is, it is not about us anyway. We go through life on our journey so afraid and focusing on stuff and things and people that really don't matter in the end. At what point in our life do we actually come to the conclusion and realize for our own selves that this battle is not ours and it is not about us? How many heartaches and headaches do we have to go through to get it? We are trying to fight a battle that is not even about us anyway, because it is not our battle to fight; we are supposed to be walking our journey, minding our own business, and doing what we are supposed to do. We are not supposed to be worrying about issues and situations that we will be faced with, because GOD already told us this was going to happen. So what is the real problem? The real problem is many of us don't believe GOD, and we think that it is just something that we are doing on our very own and GOD has nothing to do with it. This is the reason the battle seems so intense to us, and many do give up, simply because we don't know. It is called lack of knowledge. The Bible tells us that, "people do perish because of lack of knowledge." Some might wonder how we get the knowledge. First of all you have to be very careful who is within your circle. If people are in your circle and they don't even know where they are going, what does this tell you? Pay attention to what people do, not what they say all the time. We only have two guidelines to follow; we will either follow GOD, or the devil, and we already know everything goes when you follow the devil, no rules apply and nothing is off limits. So if a person is not following GOD, you have your final answer, so you might not want to follow them, because you already know deep down inside what the end result will be.

Again the choice is always yours; no one can force you to do anything, without a gun to your head. So what is the excuse now! There will come a day, whether everyone believes it or not, but we will have to answer to GOD, every last one of us. Many don't believe that because they have heard all their lives that GOD is coming back, and it seems to them that it is not real because so many years have passed and they still hear the same thing. Don't be fooled. All you have to do is read your Bible; it is written. Please don't get it twisted; this is not about us, and if some of you have not figured it out yet, you might want to pay attention to what is going on around us right now. GOD's word does not lie; it is nothing but truth. There is life after death, we can believe whatever we want but we all know that nothing will stand but the TRUTH—and GOD's word is nothing but truth. Take a look around you. Have you ever wondered what happened to many of the people that you used to know? Most of them are dead. We are not here on earth to stay, we were only placed here for a time and purpose and one day it will all end, whether we want to believe it or not. Try to do what is right because it is right—because all of us will someday be gone to heaven or hell; there is no in-between. GOD is so great he gives us the opportunity to choose, so you choose. The choice is totally left up to the individual. Please make the right choice! In the end there is no one to blame but yourself, because we have the opportunity to make our own choices in whatever we decide to do.

"It's Not About Us. It Is All About Jesus. He Paid For It All!"

Chapter 13

Stop Trying to Judge People

Ladies, this is one area we really have it bad: trying to judge each other without having a clue to the real story. If we see a lady that looks better than we do, have a spouse, have more education, have a better job, car, etc. we immediately start player hating on them and trying to judge them. Who have we been dealing with that has confused our minds to think that we are not worthy and other women are? I am sick and tired of the ladies over fifty plus years old that have the nerve to try and judge women in their twenties, thirties, and even their forties, knowing that they have done every trick in the book and then some. Some have had a countless number of men and have never been married, and some have had a house full of kids and have never been married. Some have even played the game of sleeping with anybody's husband they could, but have the nerve to judge younger women just because they might have a baby out of wedlock when they have done the exact same thing, except their kids are grown now and they think no one knows that they all don't even have the same father although most of them are grown now and none of them even look alike. Stop it!

No one is perfect, so stop pretending you were perfect all your life just because you no longer can do what you use to, but now you are committed to the church. You are not fooling anyone but yourselves. Leave other women alone if you are not willing to help them and advise them in a productive and positive way. Don't talk about them and judge them; remember when you were young, what you did and who you did it too — so who are you to judge someone? They have the same tendencies that you had at those ages, so leave them alone. GOD will eventually deliver them too, just like he delivered you, if that is what they want. If the truth be told, some of you are not even delivered yet, so mind your own business. Some of you are still trying to do what you use to do at any opportunity that you get, not realizing that your season has passed. When we get older we should act older and do what older people do. Older women are suppose to be role models for younger women because everyone does not get this at home. There will always be someone watching everyone so what are you showing the world and the younger women? Believe it or not, they are definitely taking notes.

If you have lived to be half a hundred you already know nothing is new, and there probably is nothing that you haven't done or at least thought about doing. So stop trying to judge one another without knowing their story, because remember you haven't even told the truth about your story—and you think no one knows. Shame on you! But what you don't understand and realize is there are no secrets in life, and there is really nothing new, so your story will not be too much different from anyone else's; it will just be told in a different way and at a different time. Tell the truth, you cannot help anyone in life unless you are true to yourself and tell the truth about yourself, because people are not stupid—they know when you are lying. It is written all over your face that you have hatred in your heart, so this tells us a lot about your life in general; you are not really happy about what you have done over the years and now you can't take it back. If we can get pass the jealously and judging one another the world could be a better place. Ladies, we have to realize that whatever and whoever GOD has for us it is for us, and the next women cannot take it. She might try, but it will never work and she will not get it. We spend so much of our lives focusing on the wrong things and we really miss out on more than we can imagine. I do realize that all the women in the world are not like this but many are, and everywhere we go we can see it. Many of you know some within your own circle of so-called friends, whether in the church house or the clubhouse. Same type of people, just different names and faces. For the most part they all wear a disguise, because they are not sure of themselves. When you know who's you are and who you are, you don't act like that toward people because you already know that the sky is the limit for you. All you have to do is reach up and grab it. Most of the women that have those type of attitudes and jealousy in their hearts suffer from low self-esteem for some reason. Not really sure of themselves, because someone has tainted them along the way and made them feel as though they were worthless. Try your best to stay away from bitter women that don't have any goals. We should learn to leave people alone, because we don't know people; we don't even know what we are capable of doing, so stop trying to judge everyone you meet and mind your own business. Everyone can see the things that are going on in the world today; nobody ever thought that people would ever do some of the things that they have done, because we don't know what people might do. So that being said, "leave folks alone and mind your own business." Everyone has been wounded by someone they never thought would hurt them, but we have to move on; the bible tells us to count it all joy.

If we all would be honest with ourselves we would admit that: GOD is the only one who has never let us down or betrayed us.

- He has never told anyone our secrets,

- He has never promised us something and didn't give it us,

- He has never treated us like we were nobody,

- He has never talked about us behind our back,

- He has never stepped on us to give someone else the job,

- He has never forgot about us when we didn't have money and needed food to eat,

- He has never taken our kindness for weakness,

- He has never left us on a limb all by ourselves when we needed help the most,

- He has never judged us by the color of our skin,

- He has never looked at the caller ID and not answered the phone,

- He has never gotten your e-mail and not respond,

- He has never heard your cry and kept going,

- He has never just thought about himself and not about us,

- He has never gotten your blessing mixed up with anyone else's, and

- He has never left us alone.

Has anyone ever just taken the time to think about why GOD created us to live here on this earth? There has to be a purpose. It is not to be mean to each other, judge and criticize each other; this is not the purpose. Ladies, why are we so mean to each other? GOD created all of us with the same thing, it just may be stacked differently, so why are we so afraid and jealous of the next woman? Another problem we as women really have bad, when we marry or enter into a relationship with a man and he has kids. Ladies, this means he has a responsibility, "other than you," so stop acting like you are the child. Why do we try and stop men from taking care of their kids, which is their responsibility, just because we have entered into his life? This is very wrong for the women that does this. I am not saying that all women do this, but everyone knows there are some women that do. This also tells us a lot about a women who has a problem with a man taking care of his own children. Furthermore, what type of women is going to stand by any man that does not want to take care of his own children? Again, what does this say about those type of women? Ladies, you know some of you are guilty of this; stop it! It is not right! And it is not fair to the innocent children; the children are always the ones that have to suffer, and we wonder what is wrong with children today. This is not going to make that man love you any more by you not allowing him to see or take care of his own flesh and blood. You can't be that naive to think that the child's mother might actually want him back, think about it, "she had him first" and believe me there is a very strong unhealthy reason why she is not with him and "you are." You have only heard his side of the story in most cases, but if you live on and continue to stay with him I am sure you will also get the complete story someday and you will see why, "it is what it is." Also, ladies—stop trying to keep these men from seeing their children just because you and him couldn't make it together, it is wrong! every father has a right to see their own children, the children are innocent; don't take that away from the biological father, especially if this is what he really wants to do. Grow up women, let the man visit and take care of his children and he doesn't have to be with you in order to do it. Always remember, nothing is new just different names and faces. At some point in your life someone else is going to do you the same way, make sure you keep that in mind. There is no such thing as getting even with anyone, we only hurt ourselves in the end.

Ladies, stop getting upset because he no longer wants you; it's okay, he didn't deserve you anyway. That is his loss and another man's gain. Do not try to judge the lady he left you for, just remember she will be going down the same rocky road he took you down at some point and time. We have to thank GOD when a man leaves us because more than likely he was only trying to use us and take advantage of us anyway. A man truly gives us pleasure when he leaves us because we don't have to feel guilty when he runs into the quick sand down the road. Especially if he is our spouse, nothing good will come behind him, leaving us for someone else. Don't be so quick to judge women that spouses have left, you weren't there, you don't really know the entire story, so how can you judge her. There is no way any woman in their right mind is going to keep having babies by the same man if she doesn't love him when she has to know that having babies is not going to make him stay. Most men don't even know what they want, so this is the reason when they come into our lives they can make it so complicated, because most of them are never satisfied. Could it be that they don't love themselves? Or could it have anything to do with their home training or moral values, if they even have any?

Ladies, we really mess up trying to figure them out because for some reason we get fooled every single time. Don't let the well groomed, smelling good, suit wearing, slick talker fool you!! We have a bad habit of thinking that we are going to change someone, when all the time no one ends up going out of their minds but us. What on earth makes you think you are going to change someone just because they marry you, you are going to get the same thing

Ruby J. Davis

you were getting before you walked down the aisle, the only difference is, now you have a ring on your finger. How do we think we are going to make someone want us? True love does not work like that. I am sure all of us have experienced hurt in our relationships; this just goes to show us that no one perfect, and something is wrong with everyone we meet. We just don't know what it is until it is almost too late.

They seem normal, but can anyone explain normal? No, because what is normal for one person might not be normal for the next person. According to everyone we all are okay, but as we live and walk our journey we begin to realize there is no way that can be true, if no one is perfect. So stop looking for perfect people because you are not perfect. Everyone you meet and come in contact with will have flaws but who are we to judge, because we have them too — we just don't recognize them because everyone wants to appear perfect. For the ladies that think there are people with no flaws, just take off your make-up and look closely in the mirror; the mirror does not lie. The mirror just shows us the outside that is not perfect, but the inside is where most of us get fooled because no one can truly see what is deep in our hearts but GOD. We can't see your motives and agendas, but GOD knows.

True beauty comes from within, it's not always the outside and some of us don't realize this. Some of the most attractive looking women are the worst — women that you really can't stand to be around because of their bad attitudes. But can you believe they have the nerve to wonder why they have never been married? It doesn't matter how good you look on the outside, because if your attitude is not right you are totally messed up, and often don't even realize it. How quickly are we fooled; but all you have to do is check yourself. Everything starts with ourselves, it is called self-examination, and nobody can do that better than you. Stop the judging and do whatever it is that you're supposed to do, because if you do that, you don't have time to worry about why other people do what they do. It's not your concern anyway. Most of us while walking on this journey, do whatever we have to do to make it and leave the judging to GOD. The last time I checked that was GOD's job, not anyone else's, because he knew we didn't have enough sense to do it.

"Always Remember God Does Not Discriminate, The Devil Does Not Discriminate, And Trial And Tribulations Do Not Discriminate. Everyone Gets Equal Opportunity In Those Areas!"

Chapter 14

GOD IS LOVE

Ladies, if nothing else, we know that GOD is Love. The following list contains **RED FLAGS and WARNING SIGNS** that we need to run from when evaluating a relationship with a man, because more than likely he is running some sort of game — even though he doesn't realize he is actually just **playing himself**. These are examples of when men really think that we, as women, are completely desperate and stupid!!!

If he:

- Only calls you Monday through Thursday
- Never talks on the phone but always just text messages you
- Doesn't tell you where he lives
- Hasn't taken you ANYWHERE in public
- Only calls you late at night
- Never has anything to talk about
- Wears a wedding band but says he is not married
- Never offers to do something nice for you
- Claims he works all day everyday and never gets a day off
- Can't ever take you on a real date
- Only wants to come by your place
- Never invites you to his place
- Is always on the phone talking to someone else

- Never calls you on the weekend
- Never compliments you or tell you how nice you look
- Is not concerned about what you want
- Never talks about goals of any sort
- Calls you only once or twice a week
- Ignores your phone calls
- Always talking to everyone but you
- Doesn't even know what a nice date is
- Doesn't realize that you are a QUEEN
- Always going places but never offers to take you anywhere
- Doesn't realize that you can see straight through him
- Thinks, you think, that you are the only one
- Thinks he is going to make a fool out of you
- Not consistent in anything that he does
- Never offers to get your hair, nails, or pedicure done

I am sure that at some point in many of our lives we have came in contact with men like this and have dealt with them, but what a waste of time and energy it was and a setback in our life. These men have been running games all their lives; many of them are single and probably never married and never will be, but they sometimes have the nerve to wonder why. If we fall for these type of guys, we don't really know who we are. We have to be able to recognize and spot out the devil when we see him coming or we will forever be fooled by so-called men. Everyone knows that these men do exist, and many of us have had several encounters with them, although they didn't have a clue that we didn't really want them either, because all they did was make our life a living hell and never supported anything that we wanted to do. We see them everywhere we go on a daily basis, but what they don't realize is real women can see the signs across their foreheads. They really need to know that they don't fool women, they only fool themselves. I was always taught to give men a rope because more than likely he will hang himself. "Who taught me that?" The men!!! At what point do men stop playing teenage games and think that we women are so desperate that we can't see what they are trying to do to us? This is how innocent people get hurt; don't do to people what you don't want done to you. We don't see on the news how men and women's lives have been taken constantly for playing games; these are some of the untold stories, but we need to know that they do exist!

Ladies, if we are still falling for this type of man, then we really don't realize how we are bringing drama and trouble into our own home for no reason whatsoever. These are nothing but over grown boys that need to be left right where they are at, which is in denial, because they will swear up and down that they are real men because they wear pants. Run! This is nothing but a set-up from the devil and you already know this because you have meet so many with the same worn-out routine. Remember: nothing is new, just new faces, new addresses and new names. This type of man doesn't want anything from us but our "pride and joy," which they do not deserve, so stop giving them the time of the day. They don't even deserve your beautiful smile, just keep on going, because trust me when I say, they don't want nothing. Please don't think that you can change them, let them go on down the road with those old games and tricks that they think we are not aware of. Somewhere down the line throughout their lives they missed a lot, but they are not even aware of it; just pray for them that GOD will some day deliver them and move on. Don't waste your time trying to figure out what is wrong with them or thinking that you are a pro and you will be that woman who will change them; you will die trying. Leave them alone; it is much, much deeper than what you see.

If you are still willing to deal with them, be prepared for the dead-end consequences and setbacks in your life or even death. He is not worth that, he doesn't have anything but himself to offer you which you really don't want because he is not even all of that, he just thinks he is because he is in disguise.

For the women that are already trapped by men like this, praying is your only option, don't fool yourself! I know you probably didn't even see him coming but just pray, because you cannot change the devil, this is GOD's job. Many of us have heard almost all our lives, "always pay attention to how a man treats his mother!" But what if his mother is dead? If his mother is dead, you better fast and pray and let GOD reveal to you the things that he would have never told you. Ladies, these are some of the real life valley experiences that we have been enduring through our journey, being fooled by what was supposed to be a real man. If the truth be told, many of these men have made our lives miserable, and we know that this is true and this has caused our journey to be more exhausted and out of control than it was suppose to be. If we didn't pray, many of us would be spending our life in prison, and we all know why, so don't even act like you don't. Everyone that is living has a heart, which means we all have feeling of some sort. Just be careful how you treat people, no one can fool anyone — they just think they can, but all we have to do is read a few death certificates.

We must pay attention to the red flags ladies, if you know you can't see GOD in him, guess what? He is not of GOD! It is that simple. Stop trying to make your life complicated when it doesn't have to be. Just pay attention to the signs that GOD gives us and you can't go wrong because it is what it is. If it sounds like a game, it is a game; if he looks like a crook, he is a crook, and if it sounds like a lie, it is a lie — and the list goes on. These are the kind of men who will mess your mind up for life if you let them. Take a trip to the psychiatric hospital and you'll see for yourselves the damages done to women. So what does this tell us about half-grown men? At what point do we get it? We lose our minds and go completely crazy over someone who doesn't even want us! GOD please help us! Show us women the true light... before it is too late.

"WE CAN DO BAD ALL BY OURSELVES."

Summary

What a journey this is. We have to truly acknowledge and recognize how good our GOD is. We are all traveling on a journey and many of us don't have a clue as to where we are going. The trials and tribulations that we are faced with are all in GOD's plan. He knew we needed them in order to know and get us closer to him, so this is why he allows them to arise in our lives. But we must keep in mind that they are not to kill or destroy us, but just to make us stronger and better. Remember: GOD is with us always, which mean we can lean and depend on him and we can get through the bad times just like we do the good. We can't possibly think that times were meant to always be good; we have to be realistic. If times were always good all the time, there would be no need for GOD. But remember GOD is a jealous GOD; he doesn't want to be left out either. Keep in mind when you are going through your storms of life, GOD is with you and he has everything under his control. It might not always seem that way because we may think that it is something that we are doing, but it is not. If GOD allows it to come our way he knows we are capable of dealing with it without us losing our minds, with him by our side. So stop panicking and getting all bent out of shape just because nothing seems to be going "your way." Just remember who has the Master's plan and remember that the Master's plan overrides our plans every time.

Ladies, if we take a look at our lives we can see the choices that we made. It is time for us to stop blaming other people for our mistakes and stand up to the consequences like real women. No one ever told us that this road was going to be easy, everyone always just assumed that because they really never knew what the next person had to go through to get to where they are. But we have met so many people that have traveled this journey, still standing and making it—and so can we. Nothing is new under the sun, so we should be able to make it; others did. It is time to stop making all these unwise choices just to be accepted by men. If they don't want us we can't make them want us. Move on; GOD has someone for everyone, and if you found the wrong sort, he is not yours anyway, so let that headache go and move on with your life and let a real man find you, just like the Bible tells us. "He that finds a wife, finds a good thing." All women are worthy of nothing but the best. Many of us just jumped out there in our flesh, allowing men to taint us so very badly, but now we must heal before trying to move on.

Ladies, it is healing time. If you have gotten to your last straw and you know you are completely done with him, stay single and let those wounds heal; you will not have a healthy relationship until then. If you decide to just jump right into another relationship, you will be wrecking your life along with someone else's, so don't do it! Just wait, it is not the end of the world; whoever GOD has for you, he is for you and nobody else will get him, so just relax! Take your time and heal before trying to move on; you need to try it, it really works. Save yourself the headaches and heartaches that you don't have to endure. Remember nothing is new, it is same game, he just has a different name, a different face, and different addresses, so watch out! Be careful, because we all know what he really wants; he knows your heart has been broken, so he knows you have open wounds—all he wants to do is continue to throw salt on them and move on to the next victim, and then turn around and call you crazy. Don't fall for that; you've already been there and done that—more than likely more than once, and we all know what the end result was. We should have grown beyond this point in our lives ladies, these are games for the teenagers coming along to play who really don't know any better—but we should know better. Grow Up! So what is the real problem? Well, the number one real problem is no one likes to be alone and this is why we are so messed up, because no one wants to take the time to heal. Some of us don't love ourselves, because if we did we would not be so anxious to have a man so fast, knowing that we are stilling hurting from the last series of trauma events from previous men. Therefore we will never get on the right track, being anxious and continually doing the same thing, but always looking for different results. So ladies, stop being angry at all the women that you come in contact with who have actually come to their senses and no longer do the same thing looking for different results; just do what they did.

Living a celibate life is the best option any women can choose when she is single, because the only drama she has to deal with is her own. Try it, it will not kill you; it will only make you stronger. This also gives us the time and space that we need to heal from those unfit, unhealthy, heartbreaking, overwhelming, traumatizing, dramatic past relationships. Because ladies, we all have to admit there are some men out there that will make you lose your mind if you allow them too. This happens because most of them really don't know who or what they want, so they make our lives complicated because they wait until they have actually already lied to us before they really show us who they are. And they will turn around ignore you, act as if you don't exist and leave you hanging out there to dry, and tell everyone else you were a crazy woman. So if you have already been through the storms with men, what are you waiting for to actually have peace in your life, because you will never get peace until you decide to do it the right way. Stop acting crazy; we all know the right way to do things — we just feel that it takes too long. Ladies, stop being so phony and face life the way it is. He doesn't want you, so leave him alone and stop being anxious for something that is not even worth having.

You get out of life according to the choices that you make. Keep this in mind when you realize you aren't making the right choices. Please be prepared for the setbacks and consequences that come along with it. And guess what! Now you will have to start all over again, when all of it could have been avoided. In order to get beyond your past you have to do something that you have never done, to get something you have never had — which is to do it the right way: you will see the difference. We already know the type of people that don't have our best interest at heart, so don't waste your time trying to explain anything to people; we only have to answer to GOD. Who really cares what people think of us and what we do, only we know what we really have to do, so just do it, and remember: it is not about us anyway, so don't take it personally.

There are times in our life we have to wonder, what are we doing here on earth? There is a reason and a purpose for everyone, although many of us never come to that conclusion because we spend so much time in unfit, unhealthy, heartbreaking, dramatizing relationships and we can't even think straight. For this reason many of us will never know why we are here, because many of us have lost our minds and we can't think clearly. What it really is, some may think they know but do they really know? This is a question that many can't and will not answer directly, but they will say, you will know so we have to believe that. I do believe that GOD reveals everything to us in his timing, but it would be wise to say some of us do miss it. If you live a very busy lifestyle, face it, you are not really communicating with GOD to get proper instructions. There is such a thing as too much chaos in one's life and people who run their lives like that don't even know if they are going or coming — so how are they hearing from GOD? Many of us do try to take on too many tasks at one time. But why? That is the question. Is it really worth you living a whole lifetime and not have a clue as to why you were ever here on earth in the first place? Many have gone on and completed their journey and did absolutely nothing, But again, why? It can be very confusing when you come in contact with people that have lived to be over sixty years old and you ask them if they know their purpose and they can't respond because they don't have an answer — and they are so afraid to say no. If you don't know, you just don't know, but I think it is our job to find out what it is. As long as we are seeking GOD for it, he will eventually show us. So does this mean that people who don't seek GOD for it just don't care to know? Many are just existing here on earth and they truly act like they love it, but they don't have a clue to what really is going on. WOW!

Watch out for the devil; he is always in different disguises because we know that GOD is love. Ladies, if we are not getting real love from these men, they are not of GOD. It is that simple! Please don't spend your life miserable, mean, and mad because you are sleeping with the devil when you really don't have too. Just remember: it is what it is and don't try and change it. Just do something about it, because remember, you chose him. Without GOD we don't have the sense that we think we have; we always end up choosing the devil—but GOD chooses us.

"PLEASE KEEP IN MIND EVERYTHING THAT WE HAVE TO ENDURE IS ALL FOR GOD'S GLORY!"

www.ingramcontent.com/pod-product-compliance
Lightning Source LLC
Chambersburg PA
CBHW031215270326
41931CB00006B/571